The District Railway

The Metropolitan District Railway was incorporated on 29 July 1864, but was invariably referred to as the District Railway in order to avoid confusion with its senior neighbour. The District opened its section between South Kensington and Westminster on 24 December 1868, Blackfriars being reached on 30 May 1870 and Mansion House on 3 July 1871. The Metropolitan itself extended eastwards from Farringdon Street to Aldgate by 18 November 1876 and on to Tower Hill by 25 September 1882, the master plan being for the Metropolitan and the District to work together to achieve the completion of the Inner Circle.

However, progress with the Inner Circle was frequently interrupted by squabbles between the two companies. One source of friction was that services on the District were initially worked by the Metropolitan, and the terms of the working agreement favoured the latter. The District's obvious course of action was to purchase its own locomotives, and the first of its own Beyer Peacock 4-4-0Ts was delivered in July 1871. Despite the poor relations between the two companies, the final section of the Inner Circle was eventually completed and was unveiled to the public on 6 October 1884.

While work on the Inner Circle was under way, the District opened, on 1 June 1877, a con-nection at Hammersr_____ operation of services between _____ mond. The District' _____ opened on 1 July 18__ Brompton to Putne__ and the route to _____ throughout on 21 July __

It is said that imitation is the sincerest form of flattery, and in terms of motive power the District Railway followed the lead of the Metropolitan. The District opted for Beyer Peacock 4-4-0Ts which were very similar to the Met's locomotives, the only real differences being Stirling-style chimneys, and weatherboards which were bent slightly backwards over the footplate. The first 24 4-4-0Ts cost the District £2,280 apiece, but the later ones cost £2,633 each. The District took delivery of 54 such locomotives, Nos 1-24 being built in 1871, Nos 25-30 in 1876, Nos 31-36 in 1881, Nos 37-42 in 1883, Nos 43-48 in 1884 and Nos 49-54 in 1886. It should, however, be pointed out that, for the first batch, letters were initially used instead of numbers. The District used a dull green livery for its locomotives, but brand-new No 36 wore photographic grey for its official picture in 1881.
Ian Allan Library

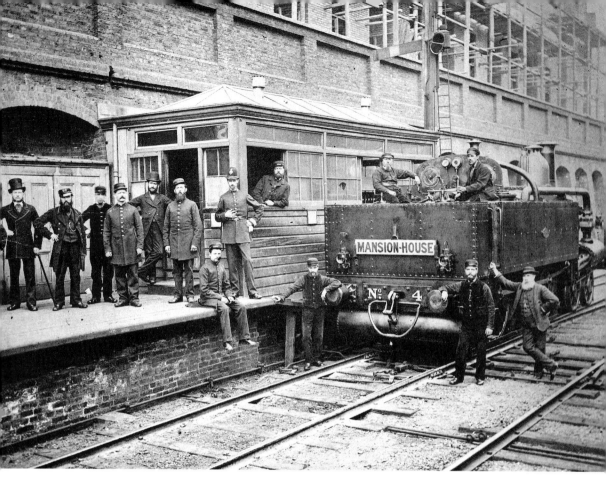

Above left:
In this superb picture, District Railway 4-4-0T No 4 shows off its bunker at Earls Court in May 1876. The old signal cabin will undoubtedly be of interest to signalling enthusiasts.
Ian Allan Library

Above:
District Railway No 20, built in 1871.
Bucknall Collection/Ian Allan Library

Below left:
District Railway No 10 poses at West Brompton in May 1876.
Ian Allan Library

Below:
The number of this District 4-4-0T is partly obscured, but it has been suggested that it is No 16 of 1871.
Bucknall Collection/Ian Allan Library

The City Widened Lines

The increasing use of the Metropolitan's tracks between King's Cross and Farringdon Street, the potential usefulness of a terminus almost in the heart of the City, and the need to provide proper access to Smithfield meat market were the main motives behind the construction of what have always been known as the 'Widened Lines'. The plans for the Widened Lines involved the quadrupling of the section between King's Cross and Farringdon Street by means of a second tunnel through Clerkenwell, a wrought-iron bridge, known as the 'Ray Street Gridiron', being needed on the approach to Farringdon Street where a new station was constructed slightly to the east of the old one. An extension of the original line eastwards to Moorgate Street was also included in the masterplan, that being completed on 23 December 1865. The Widened Lines themselves were opened in a piecemeal fashion: the first stretch was unveiled in March 1866 but the last section was not ready for passenger usage until 17 February 1868.

As soon as the Widened Lines opened throughout, passenger services commenced, although the first cross-London freight trains had run on 20 February 1866. On 13 July 1868 the Midland Railway started directing its passenger services to and from Bedford over the Widened Lines into Moorgate Street. As St Pancras station was at that time not quite completed, Moorgate Street therefore claimed the distinction of being the Midland's first terminus in London. From 1 July 1869 the GWR also used the Widened Lines for access to Smithfield, but those were standard gauge workings as broad gauge services on the Metropolitan had ceased on 15 March.

Above right:
The City Widened Lines and connections at King's Cross, *circa* **1870.**

Below right:
The City Widened Lines and connections in the Farringdon Street and Moorgate Street areas.

Below:
The original wrought-iron bridge carrying the Metropolitan's King's Cross-Moorgate Street line over the Widened Lines at the 'Ray Street Gridiron' is evident in this illustration which appeared in the *Illustrated Times* **of 27 February 1868. The bridge also acted as a strut between the walls of the cutting. Its girders were renewed in 1892 and the whole structure was replaced by a form of concrete raft in 1960.**
London Transport

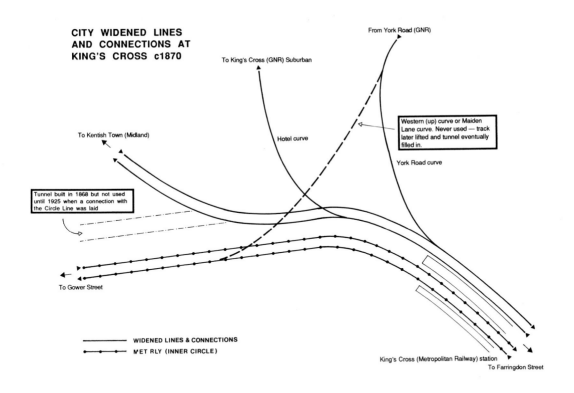

CITY WIDENED LINES AND CONNECTIONS AT KING'S CROSS c1870

From York Road (GNR)

To King's Cross (GNR) Suburban

To Kentish Town (Midland)

Hotel curve

Western (up) curve or Maiden Lane curve. Never used — track later lifted and tunnel eventually filled in.

York Road curve

Tunnel built in 1868 but not used until 1925 when a connection with the Circle Line was laid

To Gower Street

WIDENED LINES & CONNECTIONS

MET RLY (INNER CIRCLE)

King's Cross (Metropolitan Railway) station

To Farringdon Street

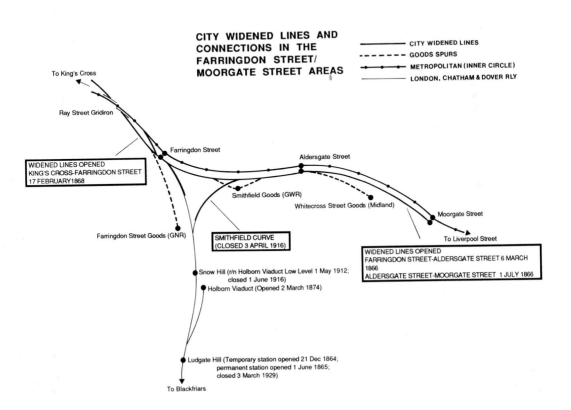

CITY WIDENED LINES AND CONNECTIONS IN THE FARRINGDON STREET/ MOORGATE STREET AREAS

CITY WIDENED LINES

GOODS SPURS

METROPOLITAN (INNER CIRCLE)

LONDON, CHATHAM & DOVER RLY

To King's Cross

Ray Street Gridiron

Farringdon Street

Aldersgate Street

WIDENED LINES OPENED KING'S CROSS-FARRINGDON STREET 17 FEBRUARY 1868

Smithfield Goods (GWR)

Whitecross Street Goods (Midland)

Moorgate Street

To Liverpool Street

Farringdon Street Goods (GNR)

SMITHFIELD CURVE (CLOSED 3 APRIL 1916)

WIDENED LINES OPENED FARRINGDON STREET-ALDERSGATE STREET 6 MARCH 1866 ALDERSGATE STREET-MOORGATE STREET 1 JULY 1866

Snow Hill (r/n Holborn Viaduct Low Level 1 May 1912; closed 1 June 1916)

Holborn Viaduct (Opened 2 March 1874)

Ludgate Hill (Temporary station opened 21 Dec 1864; permanent station opened 1 June 1865; closed 3 March 1929)

To Blackfriars

Top:
The GWR's freight workings through the Widened Lines were, for a while, entrusted to a pair of Wolverhampton-built 0-6-0Ts, Nos 643/44. The locomotives were part of a class of 12 built in 1871/72 with 4ft 6½in diameter wheels, 16in x 24in cylinders and weights of 34tons 12cwt. Nos 643/44 were fitted with condensing apparatus from new, the latter engine losing its fitments in 1884, while four other members of the class, Nos 633/34/41/42, were fitted with condensing gear when reboiled in later years. The locomotive in the photograph, No 634, underwent reboilering in 1895 and, it is believed, retained its condensing pipes until withdrawal in 1934 although, to the very end, its crews had no more protection than the weatherboard seen in the picture.
Bucknall Collection/Ian Allan Library

Above:
The first new Great Northern Railway 0-4-4WTs to be officially allocated to duties through the Widened Lines and via Snow Hill were Nos 621-28 of Stirling's '120' class of 1872, although it seems that other members of the class were fitted with the necessary condensing equipment at various times. An interesting feature was the use of a revolving destination board, seen on the rear of No 625's bunker.
Ian Allan Library

Top right:
One of the GNR's original condensing '120' class 0-4-4WTs was No 628, seen here after its reboilering of 1896.
Ian Allan Library

Bottom right:
The Midland Railway's first locomotives for subterranean work in London were a batch of 10 2-4-0Ts, built by Beyer Peacock in 1868. They were quickly found to be unsuited to their intended duties, one of the problems being caused by the extremely rigid coupled wheelbase of 8ft 6in; after being replaced by 4-4-0Ts, they were rebuilt as tender engines. The Midland's 4-4-0Ts were built by Beyer Peacock. They were, in fact, part of an order destined for the Metropolitan, with the result that, apart from the cosmetic finish, they were virtually identical to their Met counterparts. Only six 4-4-0Ts were supplied to the Midland, where they became Nos 204-209. They were delivered towards the end of 1868 and had useful lives, all being reboiled at least once during their existences. They survived until the early 1900s, the last survivor, by then MR No 1198, being withdrawn in 1912. This magnificent picture of well-polished No 205 was almost certainly taken very early in its career.
Ian Allan Library

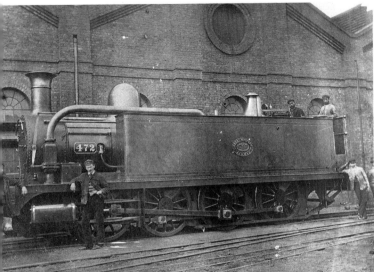

The GNR took delivery of two powerful 0-8-0Ts from the Avonside Engine Co in 1866. They had 4ft 6in diameter wheels, 18½in x 24in outside cylinders, 140lb boilers and weighed in at 56 tons apiece. Although their axle weight was only 14 tons, their wheelbase of 15ft 10in made them unsuitable for their anticipated duties of hauling coal trains to Farringdon Street or to the south of London via the LC&DR's line through Snow Hill. Therefore, the original order for six such 0-8-0Ts was cancelled, leaving just two of the machines on the GNR's books; they became Nos 472/73 and, of course, were fitted with the obligatory condensing apparatus.

Ian Allan Library

Above:

The London & North Western got in on the underground act and, in 1871/72, took delivery of 16 4-4-0Ts from Beyer Peacock. They were given Nos 2055-70 and, apart from the addition of a rear weathershield, were virtually identical to the Metropolitan's 4-4-0Ts. Ten were later rebuilt as 4-4-2Ts, and one was the subject of Francis Webb's experiments with divided drive compounds. Whether rebuilt or not, the LNWR's 4-4-0Ts all finished up on the duplicate list, No 2055 becoming duplicate No 1826 in 1885 and No 3048 in 1886. It was withdrawn in 1892.
Bucknall Collection/Ian Allan Library

Centre right:

Francis Webb's '2234' class 2-4-0Ts were condenser-fitted for London area duties. They had 4ft 8½in driving wheels and 17in x 20in cylinders, No 2250 being built in 1876 and withdrawn in 1898.
Ian Allan Library

Bottom right:

Twenty of Webb's numerous 'Motor Tanks' were condenser-fitted from new, No 761 being built in 1889 and withdrawn in 1924.
Ian Allan Library

The London, Chatham & Dover Railway

The London, Chatham & Dover Railway is not a concern usually associated with London's underground railways, but the company's connection with the Widened Lines is an integral part of the story. With the benefit of hindsight, the LC&DR can be described as an energetically ambitious company which expanded a little too fast for its own good. In the early 1860s, however, the company was branded as 'a great destroyer of house property in London', its construction schemes having required the substantial demolition of houses.

The LC&DR crossed the River Thames to Blackfriars in June 1864 and extended its line to a temporary terminus at New Bridge Street on 21 December of the same year. The permanent station at Ludgate Hill was opened on 1 June 1865, but contemporary observers were quick to remark on its unfinished state. On 1 January 1866 the LC&DR opened a trailing connection in the direction of Farringdon Street, thereby linking with the Widened Lines and providing the first and only main line through the City of London. A facing connection to Moorgate Street was opened on 1 September 1871, but remained in use only until 1916. It was not only the LC&DR which benefited from the new line as L&SWR and GNR services to Ludgate Hill were soon inaugurated, the GNR services later being extended to Victoria via Brixton. The Ludgate Hill route was used by the LC&DR for its own Herne Hill-Barnet services while, from 1869, the Midland also started operating over the line with its Hendon-Victoria trains.

Ludgate Hill station had only two platforms and, as the station was used by between 300 and 400 trains each weekday, congestion frequently resulted. It was not possible for the LC&DR to purchase the adjacent land for an extension to the station, and so a short extension was built into a new four-platform terminus, Holborn Viaduct, which opened on 2 March 1874. For services to Moorgate Street and Farringdon Road, two low-level platforms on the line below and alongside Holborn Viaduct terminus were opened on 1 August 1874; originally named Snow Hill, the through station was given its more familiar name of Holborn Viaduct (Low Level) on 1 May 1912.

In the steam era, banking assistance was usually required on the 1 in 39 climb to Holborn Viaduct (Low Level) but, in 1870, one locomotive took an uninterrupted trip down the bank. The story goes that, after experiencing problems with their engine, the crew leapt from the footplate at Ludgate Hill without having fully closed the regulator, thereby leaving the locomotive to trundle down the bank, through Farringdon Street and King's Cross (Metropolitan) before grinding to a halt in Haverstock Hill tunnel.

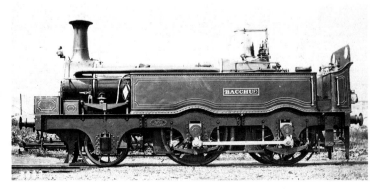

Right:
In 1872/73, the London, Chatham & Dover Railway built a quartet of 2-4-0Ts using the boilers from 4-4-0s which had been acquired in 1860/61. The 'rebuilds' kept the names of their ancestors, *Aeolus*, *Bacchus*, *Vulcan* and *Comus*, and were fitted with the necessary condensing equipment for working across London.
Bucknall Collection/Ian Allan Library

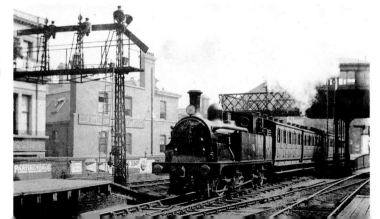

Below right:
An unidentified LC&DR 'R' class 0-4-4T is seen entering Ludgate Hill station from the south, well before the 1910 rebuilding of the station. The 'Rs' were introduced in 1891 and all were condenser-fitted; the locomotive in this picture appears to be carrying a wreath on its smokebox door, but no information is at hand as to the significance of this.
Lens of Sutton

The East London Railway

In 1865, the newly-formed East London Railway purchased the tunnel under the Thames between Wapping and Rotherhithe for £200,000. The gas-lit tunnel had been designed by Sir Marc Brunel, the father of Isambard, and had been completed in 1843 at a cost of over £600,000. Since its opening, the tunnel had been used mainly as a pedestrian thoroughfare, although fairs, which sometimes attracted some 40,000 people, had been held in the tunnel annually.

The ELR laid a railway through the tunnel and, on 7 December 1869, services commenced between New Cross (the present New Cross Gate) and Wapping (at that time named Wapping & Shadwell). They were worked by the London, Brighton & South Coast Railway, the usual steeds being Craven 0-4-4WTs and a 2-2-2T. On 11 April 1876 the line was extended to Bishopsgate Junction, near Shoreditch, on the Great Eastern Railway thereby allowing the LB&SCR to operate into Liverpool Street station. The South Eastern Railway started operating into Liverpool Street via the ELR route on 1 April 1880, a spur to the SER's line at New Cross having been provided, but the SER's services were later diverted to terminate at St Mary's, that station being suffixed 'Whitechapel Road' in 1923.

On 6 October 1884 the Metropolitan and the District jointly took over the SER's passenger services on the ELR, but the LB&SCR continued working between New Cross and Shoreditch. Freight workings on the ELR were usually entrusted to the Great Eastern which later introduced an infrequent Liverpool Street-Croydon passenger service via the line, condenser-fitted Massey Bromley 'E10' class 0-4-4Ts being the usual locomotives.

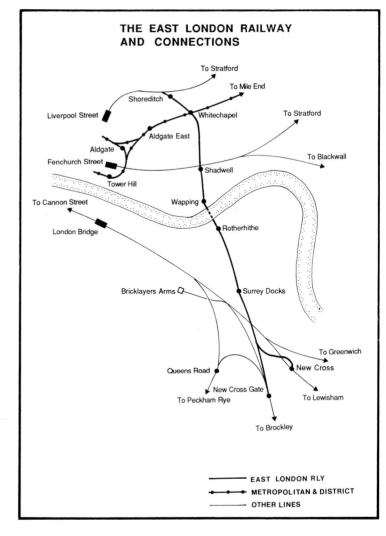

THE EAST LONDON RAILWAY AND CONNECTIONS

To Stratford
To Mile End
Shoreditch
Liverpool Street
Whitechapel
To Stratford
Aldgate East
Aldgate
Fenchurch Street
To Blackwall
Shadwell
Tower Hill
Wapping
To Cannon Street
Rotherhithe
London Bridge
Bricklayers Arms
Surrey Docks
To Greenwich
New Cross
Queens Road
New Cross Gate
To Lewisham
To Peckham Rye
To Brockley

—— EAST LONDON RLY
•—•—• METROPOLITAN & DISTRICT
—— OTHER LINES

The route of the East London Railway.

134.—EAST LONDON.

Incorporated by 28 Vic., cap. 51 (26th May, 1865), to connect by means of the Thames Tunnel the railways on the north and south of the Thames. Length, about 8 miles. Capital, 1,400,000*l.* in shares, and 466,600*l.* on mortgage.

By 29 and 30 Vic., cap. 180 (16th July, 1866), the company was authorised to construct several short branches and alter new works. Length, ¾ mile. No new capital.

By 31 and 32 Vic., cap. 163 (31st July, 1868), the company obtained various additional powers, including certain deviations and altered lines; an extension ot time till 1873, for completion of works; and confirmation of agreement with Brighton, for which, see APPENDIX to present volume.

This line commences by junctions with the Brighton, South London, South Eastern, and North Kent Railways, near New Cross, accommodating in its course the Surrey and Commercial Docks, the London Docks, and the East of London, terminates in the city, at a great terminal station in Liverpool street. There is to be a branch to the Great Eastern, and the line will pass through and accommodate the districts of New Cross, Deptford, Rotherhithe, Wapping, St. Georges-in-the-East, Limehouse, Stepney, Whitechapel, Bethnal-green, Bishopsgate, and Shoreditch. Works in progress.

CAPITAL.—The receipts and expenditure on this account to 30th June, 1868, have been as follow:—

Received.		Expended.	
Capital, 1,400,000*l.*, in 70,000 shares of 20*l.* each	£1,170,342	As per last account	£1,001,960
Interest	12,861	Land	8,357
Sale of surplus property	7,724	Construction	63,534
Transfer fees	26	Office rent, salaries, printing, and stationery, &c.	997
		Directors and auditors	1,070
		Law charges	1,846
		Parliamentary expenses	850
		Discount on shares	92,685
		Commission	123
			£1,171,425
		Cash and securities	19,528
	£1,190,954		£1,190,954

No. of Directors—12; minimum, 6; quorum, 3. *Qualification*, 50 shares of 20*l.* each.

DIRECTORS;

Chairman—WILLIAM HAWES, Esq., 17, Montague Place, Russel Square, W.C.

Lawford Ackland, Esq., Langdown Lawn, Hythe, Southampton.
James Childs, Esq., Summerfield, Putney Park Lane, Roehampton, S.W.
Major-Gen. J. S. Brownrigg, C.B., 91, Victoria Street, Westminster, S.W.
Peter Graham, Esq., Queen's Road, Regent's Park, N.W.
John Sale Barker, Esq., 11, Palace Gardens Terrace, Kensington, W.
Alfred Smee, Esq., F.R.S., Finsbury Circus, London, E.C.

OFFICERS.—Sec., G. E. Cooper; Eng., John Hawkshaw, C.E.; Auditors, H. M. Brownrigg and H. H. Stansfeld; Solicitors, Wilson, Bristows, and Carpmael, 1, Copthall Buildings; Surveyor and Valuer, E. N. Clifton; Bankers, The London and Westminster Bank.

Offices—3, Great Winchester Street Buildings, E.C.

The corporate details of the East London Railway were given in *Bradshaw's Shareholders' Guide* for 1869.

Below:

This illustration of an unidentifiable locomotive and train at Wapping station, at the northern end of the Thames Tunnel on the East London Railway, first appeared in the *Illustrated London News* of 8 January 1870.

London Transport

The West London Railway

With the exception of the LC&DR line from Blackfriars towards Moorgate Street and Farringdon Street, virtually all of the lines which have been listed so far have been those which finished up as part of what we know today as London's Underground system. There was, however, one important early cross-London route which was used, in part, by the Metropolitan and the District Railways but was never included in the Underground map. That was the route of the West London Railway.

The WLR ran from Kensington (Addison Road) to Willesden, where a junction was made with the London & Birmingham (later London & North Western) Railway. The WLR opened on 27 May 1844 and, although worked by the L&BR, was also used by the GWR which had taken the precaution of securing priority for its trains; of necessity, most of the line was laid with mixed gauge tracks. In March 1846 the WLR was leased jointly by the GWR and LNWR, although the line had hardly been used since the end of 1844. However, the LNWR reinstated passenger services on the WLR line in June 1862, Kensington being served by trains to and from Harrow and Camden (Chalk Farm). A continuation of the line — the West London Extension Railway — opened on 2 March 1863 to link up with the LSWR and LBSCR at or near Clapham Junction, those two companies having subscribed to the WLER's construction.

By June 1863, passenger services on the WLR/WLER were provided by all four interested parties: the LNWR trains worked between Kensington and Euston, Harrow and Camden; the GWR used the line as part of a route between Southall and Victoria; the LSWR operated between Kensington and Clapham Junction; while the LB&SCR worked from Kensington to West Croydon. Through services were offered between Euston and New Croydon, the locomotives being changed at Kensington. In later years, the Metropolitan also worked into Kensington while the District started making occasional use of the line as early as 1869, although the District's disinclination to pay a proportion of the maintenance costs of Addison Road station resulted in it being denied running powers. The GWR's services, mentioned above, continued to operate on the broad gauge until 14 March 1869.

At its peak, Kensington (Addison Road) station was remarkably well served, a total of 114 workings being accommodated each weekday in the mid-1860s, while by the mid-1870s some 200 trains worked through, or started or terminated at, the station. Initially, Addison Road station had only two platforms, but was rebuilt in 1869 with two longer platforms, both having a bay at each end.

Returning to the 'mainstream' companies which eventually made up the London Underground network, it has been seen how, in just 20 years or so after the opening of the first underground line, major foundations had already been laid for the development of the system. There was certainly no shortage of photographers to record the scene, but the limitations of contemporary camera equipment and film meant that 'action' pictures were virtually out of the question. Therefore, I apologise for the high proportion of 'static' photographs used to illustrate this period. Even the station scenes would have required exposures of many seconds, if not a minute or two.

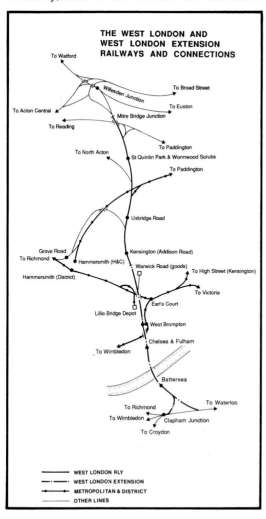

THE WEST LONDON AND WEST LONDON EXTENSION RAILWAYS AND CONNECTIONS

To Watford
Willesden Junction
To Broad Street
To Acton Central
To Euston
Mitre Bridge Junction
To Reading
To Paddington
To North Acton
St Quintin Park & Wormwood Scrubs
To Paddington
Uxbridge Road
Grove Road
To Richmond
Kensington (Addison Road)
Hammersmith (H&C)
Warwick Road (goods)
Hammersmith (District)
To High Street (Kensington)
To Victoria
Earl's Court
Lillie Bridge Depot
West Brompton
Chelsea & Fulham
To Wimbledon
Battersea
To Waterloo
To Richmond
To Wimbledon
Clapham Junction
To Croydon

——— WEST LONDON RLY
—·—·— WEST LONDON EXTENSION
•—•—• METROPOLITAN & DISTRICT
——— OTHER LINES

The West London and West London Extension Railways and connections.

2
Consolidation then electrification

The completion of the Inner Circle on 6 October 1884 was a considerable landmark in the development of London's underground railway network. For the next twenty years, steam traction reigned supreme on not only the existing network, but also many of the lines which were added to the map. Having said that, there wasn't a great deal to be appended to the list of steam-hauled services around inner London itself, the main sphere of expansionism being that of the Metropolitan Railway to the northwest of London in the semi-rural expanses of Buckinghamshire.

Metropolitan 'A' class 4-4-0T No 26 was found useful employment when floodwater affected the Widened Lines near Farringdon Street. Sadly, this splendid picture is undated.
London Transport

29

The Metropolitan Railway

The Metropolitan's dynamic chairman, Sir Edward Watkin, was keen to turn the company into a conventional main line concern. As early as 1880, the Met had reached Harrow-on-the-Hill, and subsequent extensions resulted in the company arriving at Verney Junction, 50½ miles from Baker Street, on 1 July 1892.

The extensions to Verney Junction, where the Metropolitan connected with the LNWR's Oxford-Bletchley line, had not, however, been a simple case of laying new tracks over untrodden ground. The Aylesbury-Verney Junction section had previously been the property of the GWR-worked Aylesbury & Buckingham Railway, but had been taken over by the Met on 1 July 1891. Although originally single-track, the section was doubled by 1897. Furthermore, the Met's entrance to Aylesbury from the south initially reached only a temporary station, the permanent Metropolitan/GWR joint station not being ready for its official opening until 1 January 1894.

Despite its new-found route, the Met did not inaugurate a Baker Street-Verney Junction through service until 1 January 1897. The GWR, in its capacity as joint operator of the old Aylesbury & Buckingham Railway, had protested that the Met's intended locomotives were too heavy for use beyond Aylesbury. Consequently, the Met had at first to hire two locomotives from the LNWR specially for use on that section and work it as a separate entity.

The Metropolitan Railway's Locomotive and Carriage Superintendent, J. J. Hanbury, resigned in 1893, his position being filled temporarily by T. S. Raney before the permanent appointment of T. F. Clark in 1896. A Hanbury bequest inherited by Clark was the familiar locomotive livery of maroon which had, from about 1885, replaced the plumage of unlined green. Although the maroon livery had been generally accepted as very smart, many observers nevertheless remarked that the precise shade of maroon seemed to vary considerably from year to year.

The Met's locomotive headquarters were at Neasden, extensive new workshops, a gas works and even a company 'village' having replaced the cramped locomotive headquarters at Edgware Road in 1882. During Clark's regime, one of his early experiments was to persevere with the Gibson & Lilley link motion which Hanbury had fitted to 4-4-0T No 29 in 1889. A series of comparison trials was instigated by Clark and, after the modified engine showed greater fuel economy and acceleration, all of the 4-4-0Ts were fitted with similar equipment. A further experiment involved 4-4-0T No 62 which, in 1898, was tried with Holden oil-burning equipment but, unlike most of Clark's experiments, that one was not successful.

Another railway company, which was much later to be closely linked with the Metropolitan, appeared on the scene in the late 1890s. The Great Central which until 1897 had been entitled the Manchester, Sheffield & Lincolnshire Railway,

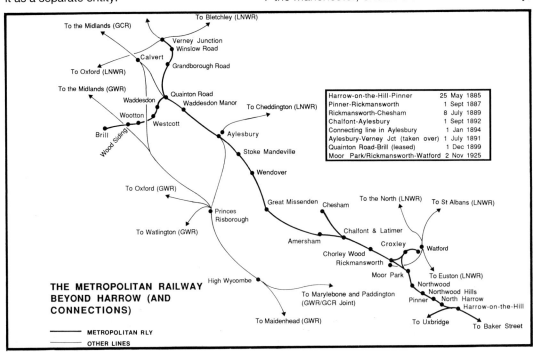

THE METROPOLITAN RAILWAY
BEYOND HARROW (AND
CONNECTIONS)

——— METROPOLITAN RLY
——— OTHER LINES

Harrow-on-the-Hill-Pinner	25 May 1885
Pinner-Rickmansworth	1 Sept 1887
Rickmansworth-Chesham	8 July 1889
Chalfont-Aylesbury	1 Sept 1892
Connecting line in Aylesbury	1 Jan 1894
Aylesbury-Verney Jct (taken over)	1 July 1891
Quainton Road-Brill (leased)	1 Dec 1899
Moor Park/Rickmansworth-Watford	2 Nov 1925

Below:

When the Metropolitan acquired the lease of the Aylesbury-Verney Junction section, the GWR, which had previously worked that section, protested that the Met's locomotives were too heavy to be used north of Aylesbury. Consequently, two 0-6-0Ts were hired from the LNWR as a stop-gap measure until the Met could take delivery of its own purpose-built lightweight locomotives. The Met's locomotives were the smart little 'D' class 2-4-0Ts, the first of which was delivered in February 1895. Built by Sharp Stewart at a cost of £1,575 each, they were very similar to four locomotives supplied in 1889/90 to the Barry Railway. The first two members of the 'D' class, Nos 71/72, were not fitted with condensing apparatus but the other four, Nos 73-76, were so equipped. Their dimensions, as recorded in the 1925 Locomotive Register, were 5ft 3in driving wheels, 17in x 24in cylinders, 800gall tanks and weights of 43tons 10cwt (condensing) or 41tons 4cwt (non-condensing). No 75 is pictured after the removal of the condensing apparatus. *London Transport*

started hauling its London-bound coal trains over the Met's tracks into Neasden on 26 July 1898. However, the GCR's use of the Met's lines for passenger services into its newly-opened terminus at Marylebone in 1899 was short-lived, running powers being transferred to the GWR route after just five days. Elsewhere to the northwest of London, the Met took a lease in December 1899 on the legendary Wotton Tramway, the exquisitely-rural branch from Quainton Road to Brill which had opened its first section in 1871 and had been completed the following year.

One of the condenser-fitted 'D' class 2-4-0Ts, No 76, circa 1900.
Bucknall Collection/Ian Allan Library

Metropolitan Railway 4-4-0T No 46 was one of the last members of the 'A' class to be built. In this picture, it models the Hanbury maroon livery of 1885.
Ian Allan Library

Above:
When the Metropolitan extended its 'main line' deeper and deeper into Buckinghamshire it was considered that additional locomotives would be required to augment the 4-4-0Ts on the longer runs. Consequently, four 0-4-4Ts were ordered from Neilsons of Glasgow at a cost of £2,200 each and were delivered in 1891. Carrying Nos 67-70, the 0-4-4Ts became designated the 'C' class. Their design leant heavily on that of James Stirling's 0-4-4Ts for the South Eastern Railway, and they were the first Met locomotives to be fitted with full cabs from new. All four were rebuilt in 1901-03, coal rails being added to the bunkers and new chimneys being fitted.
Bucknall Collection/Ian Allan Library

Bottom right:
The seven Metropolitan 'E' class 0-4-4Ts were Nos 1 and 77-82, the first number having become available in December 1897 when its original carrier, a Beyer Peacock 'A' class 4-4-0T, was scrapped after an accident. Designed by the Met's Superintendent, Thomas Clark, the first three members of the 'E' class were constructed at Neasden whereas the others were built by Hawthorn Leslie at a cost of £3,392 each. Delivered in a piecemeal manner between 1896 and 1901, the 'Es' basic dimensions, as recorded in 1925, were 5ft 6in driving wheels, 17in x 26in cylinders (17½in diameter for the Hawthorn Leslie engines), 1,300gal tanks and weights of 54tons 10cwt. Their tractive effort at 85% was a useful 16,400lb. Here, No 77 provides ample evidence that the Verney Junction section was not always treated to the most modern rolling stock.
Bucknall Collection/Ian Allan Library

Left:

A pair of Peckett 'X' class 0-6-0STs were purchased by the Metropolitan Railway; they had 3ft 10in wheels, 16in x 22in cylinders, 1,160gall tanks and weighed 39tons apiece. The first, Works No 664, was delivered in 1897 and became Met No 101. Its designated duty was shunting work at Harrow and so there was no need for it to be fitted with condensing apparatus. The goods yard at Harrow was, in fact, jointly owned by the Met and the Great Central, the arrangement being that each of the two companies would work the yard for alternating five-year periods.
Ian Allan Library

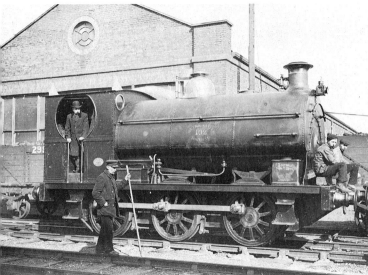

Centre left:

The second of the two Peckett 0-6-0STs, Works No 823, was delivered to the Metropolitan in 1899. Carrying Met No 102, it was intended for shunting duties at Harrow and Neasden and so, like its classmate, did not need condensing gear. Although some sources refer to the two Pecketts as being designated the 'S' class by the Metropolitan, no such classification seems to have been officially applied.
Bucknall Collection/Ian Allan Library

Above:
Although the branch from Quainton Road to Brill never became part of the Underground network, it nevertheless warrants inclusion in this book. Operations on the Brill branch, which the Metropolitan took over in 1899, were somewhat different to the hustle and bustle just 40-odd miles away in Central London. Prior to the Met's takeover of the branch, eighteen-year-old Manning Wardle 0-6-0T *Huddersfield*, a former contractor's engine, had been purchased in 1894 for use on the line but, perhaps unsurprisingly, the locomotive failed to curry favour with the Met and was disposed of before too long. This 'pre-Met' scene at Quainton Road shows *Huddersfield* with the original Oxford & Aylesbury Tramroad coach and a later bogie vehicle.
Ian Allan Library

Below:
This glimpse of pre-Metropolitan life on the Wotton Tramway (the Brill branch) shows Aveling & Porter locomotive, Works No 846, at Quainton Road. The machine was purchased in June 1872, a similar contraption having been bought in January that year. In an 1889 audit, the combined value of both engines was put at £130. They worked on the line until the early 1890s but were sold for £25 the pair about 1897 and consequently missed becoming Metropolitan stock by only a couple of years. The one in the picture was soon cannibalised to provide spares for its companion, Works No 807, which was later preserved.
Ian Allan Library

Life on the Brill branch was slightly more tranquil that at the other end of the Metropolitan's operations. Sadly, this picture is undated but it was clearly taken well before 1911 when the Met relaid the line and provided standard-height platforms.
Ian Allan Library

Above:
When the Metropolitan inherited the Brill branch, part of the legacy was Manning Wardle 'K' class 0-6-0ST *Wotton No 2* which, although built only in 1899, was sold to contractors within a few years of the Met's take over. Here, the locomotive is seen at the branch terminus at Brill — note the initials 'MR' on its buffer beam.
Lens of Sutton

Left:
After the more extensive upgrading of the Brill branch in 1911, heavier locomotives could be accommodated, and 'A' class 4-4-0Ts Nos 23 and 41 became the regular branch engines. Here, No 23 is seen at Westcott.
Lens of Sutton

The District Railway

Initially, it had been widely assumed that the District Railway would be absorbed by the Metropolitan Railway, the Metropolitan itself being one concern which viewed absorption as almost inevitable. By the mid-1880s, however, the District had become well established as a totally independent company.

The District inaugurated its services to Wimbledon on 3 June 1889, the LSWR's Wimbledon services via Putney not commencing until 1 July. Elsewhere, the District's goods services on the short branch to South Acton commenced on 15 May 1899, although passenger workings were not introduced until the days of electrification. On 28 June 1903, the Ealing-South Harrow section opened throughout and, on 4 July 1904, the branch from Harrow-on-the-Hill to Uxbridge (Belmont Road) was opened, working being undertaken by Metropolitan steam locomotives for the first six months. The Met formally took over the line on 1 July 1905.

On the Uxbridge branch, a station named Park Royal & Twyford Abbey was built to serve the new Royal Show Ground, but was closed in 1931 when the new Park Royal station was unveiled. Elsewhere on the branch, open platforms were provided at Ickenham in 1905 but, in wet weather, the public took to sheltering under a bridge alongside the track and so £80 was begrudgingly spent on wooden shelters.

Elsewhere in the District's area, the original station at Hounslow Town closed in March 1886 but was reopened in March 1903, only to be replaced by a new station on the Hounslow Barracks (Hounslow West) line in May 1909. In the east of London, a connection between Whitechapel and the London, Tilbury & Southend Railway at Campbell Road Junction in Bow opened on 2 June 1902.

Right:
Even in their later years, the District Railway's locomotives were invariably very well turned out. Here, one of the 1880 batch, No 34, poses outside the company's depot at Lillie Bridge.
Bucknall Collection/Ian Allan Library

Below:
No excuses are offered for using another splendid picture of a District Railway 4-4-0T, this time No 53. The caption supplied with this 1905 picture states: 'George Spiller, centre' — perhaps descendants of Mr Spiller are around today?
Ian Allan Library

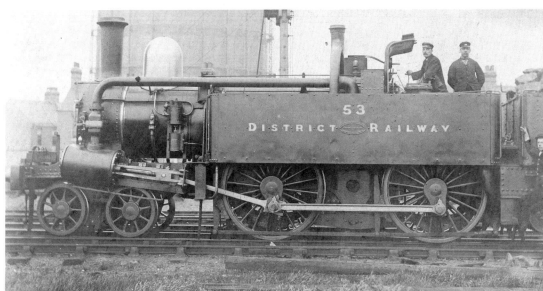

Above:
The District Railway's services to Wimbledon commenced on 3 June 1889, but it is uncertain whether this picture of Beyer Peacock 4-4-0T No 4 was taken to mark the inauguration of the service.
Bucknall Collection/Ian Allan Library

Below:
The old and the new pose alongside each other, allegedly at Hammersmith; District Railway 4-4-0T No 16 of 1871 on the right and original electric stock of 1903 on the left.
Bucknall Collection/Ian Allan Library

Electrification

By the end of the nineteenth century, the hint of electrification had become increasingly strong, the first electric-powered 'tube' railway under London having been unveiled in 1890. Back in 1882, the Metropolitan had obtained powers to convert to electric traction on the Inner Circle while the District had, in 1888, considered the possibility of battery locomotives, but endless hostilities between the Met and the District had, for some time, put paid to any chance of an agreement. Instead, the District took the lead when, in 1901, it came under the control of Charles Tyson Yerkes, an American businessman who was a keen proponent of electrified railways. The Metropolitan, with injured pride, had little option but to follow the lead set by its smaller rival. It was the beginning of the end for steam's domination under London. Electrification was carried out at such a pace that, by November 1906, steam had been ousted south of Willesden Green on the Metropolitan's Baker Street-Aylesbury 'main line'. In July 1908, Harrow became the change over point from steam to electric traction.

In 1909, the idea for the Underground as we know it today was formulated by Albert Stanley, the master plan being to encompass the electrified lines of the District and Metropolitan in the inner suburbs and Central London. The District was happy with the prospect of being an integral part of a new system, but the Metropolitan made no secret that it would have preferred total independence.

By the end of 1906 the Metropolitan had handed over its steam services on the East London Railway to the South Eastern & Chatham, and this rendered even more steam locomotives redundant. The obvious candidates for disposal were the older 4-4-0Ts and around 3,000 sale catalogues were circulated to advertise the availability of these stalwarts, some of the catalogues going as far away as China. By the end of 1908, however, only a few of the locomotives had found new homes. As far as can be ascertained, that sales campaign resulted in the Met selling only ten of the 4-4-0Ts in working order. They comprised six (Nos 10/11/12/13/15/66) which went to Cambrian Railways for a price of £3,500 for the lot, two (Nos 20/34) to the newly-opened Nidd Valley Light Railway in Yorkshire, one (No 37) to the reconstituted West Somerset Mineral Railway, and another (No 61) for departmental duties on the Mersey Railway.

Predictably, the District Railway also found itself with a surplus of steam locomotives and most were soon scrapped. It is believed that, after 1906, only Nos 27/33-36/38/39 remained in action and, of those, all but Nos 33/34/38 were cut up before very long, their final duties having been on ballast trains.

The hamlet of Roadwater on the Brendon Hills in West Somerset is hardly an integral part of the story of London's railways, but this picture is nevertheless well worth including. One of the Metropolitan Railway 4-4-0Ts which found a new home after being displaced by electrification was No 37 of 1881. The locomotive's new owner was the reconstituted West Somerset Mineral Railway which reopened in 1907, and No 37 certainly proved to be a major attraction when it lined up for the photographer on 3 July, the day before the recommencement of services between Watchet and Comberow.
Bert Hole

REVENUE AND EXPENDITURE.

Year.	1st Half.			2nd Half.		
	Receipts.	Expenditure.	Balance available for Dividend.	Receipts.	Expenditure.	Balance available for Dividend.
	£	£	£	£	£	£
1882	330,883	113,085	117,263	338,616	111,247	118,176
1883	350,577	118,342	118,688	358,455	122,225	119,478
1884	357,358	122,259	120,007	383,064	128,574	135,909
1885	363,173	132,944	114,312	370,284	126,277	123,876
1886	404,259	132,568	161,630	374,805	134,161	168,305
1887	365,474	132,023	158,513	360,617	131,036	126,865
1888	372,232	132,462	126,941	374,953	134,527	127,447
1889	380,556	139,918	128,096	382,578	144,249	119,648
1890	384,293	141,627	121,737	391,859	144,068	121,831
1891	403,575	145,916	130,513	406,702	151,314	129,784
1892	408,922	152,497	130,834	407,995	151,396	128,649
1893	409,551	150,340	124,394	395,480	152,021	100,527
1894	420,300	160,119	116,624	409,536	155,440	116,423
1895	416,844	159,983	122,142	424,740	162,182	126,035
1896	434,396	164,342	133,706	440,675	167,656	137,924
1897	461,355	175,684	151,746	464,231	180,103	152,480
1898	468,883	182,590	152,119	477,139	185,944	161,065
1899	486,425	188,872	166,350	490,581	199,149	162,125
1900	493,709	201,087	161,901	472,438	212,462	128,594
1901	462,349	208,446	121,539	459,904	208,995	120,047
1902	463,594	207,496	121,073	484,960	208,975	129,598
1903	482,685	211,252	134,215	502,403	207,779	143,584
1904	504,535	207,842	143,526	513,912	214,129	133,579
1905	506,195	216,686	112,403	503,844	214,952	110,595
1906	468,562	213,032	82,971	439,024	197,874	56,465
1907	437,399	193,361	53,937	448,362	191,959	56,159
1908	454,782	199,780	54,316	480,300	202,044	62,638
1909	464,857	193,243	68,877	482,530	205,654	70,900
1910	481,689	194,020	78,182	497,344	200,148	88,802
1911	496,702	195,667	101,039	497,808	195,789	95,686
1912	484,372	191.462	89,387	503,487	194,550	102,350

The cost of electrification had a marked effect on the Metropolitan's *(above)* and the District's *(below)* finances. The sharp dips in both companies' pecuniary health around 1905, as seen in these figures, were due to the expenditure on electrification. The statistics are taken from *Bradshaw's Shareholders' Guide* for 1915.

REVENUE AND EXPENDITURE.

Year.	1st Half.			2nd Half.		
	Receipts.	Expenditure.	Balance available for Preference Dividend.	Receipts.	Expenditure.	Balance Available for Preference Dividend.
	£	£	£	£	£	£
1873	113,396	55,660	8,030	101,937	62,122	..
1874	117,039	53,535	15,205	115,932	57,362	7,652
1875	137,228	66,895	18,860	135,693	62,665	23,095
1876	149,248	68,696	30,790	134,155	64,638	22,736
1877	151,815	66,853	37,982	144,689	64,103	34,238
1878	161,642	70,490	44,661	151,059	67,813	37,984
1879	166,506	68,399	52,503	165,925	71,150	94,775
1880	186,269	79,243	54,762	176,638	81,740	46,237
1881	194,960	83,363	51,776	178,065	87,176	37,670
1882	190,409	88,355	41,734	176,475	81,718	37,536
1883	198,802	85,860	49,747	202,504	85,819	38,027
1884	205,415	86,196	39,873	212,563	97,640	30,492
1885	205,309	98,056	15,167	210,926	98,531	19,266
1886	210,353	100,718	16,293	220,112	97,224	27,002
1887	203,953	96,421	19,768	181,691	95,375	26,537
1888	191,296	93,241	2,261	189,916	91,408	10,232
1889	188,225	91,184	7,181	185,844	92,665	6,132
1890	200,405	93,569	21,433	194,038	95,606	17,512
1891	213,023	94,714	18,750	207,340	98,273	19,827
1892	216,539	95,818	27,883	..	..	..
1893	209,302	95,507	20,872	200,383	97,810	11,506
1894	221,906	98,739	29,630	204,874	99,326	11,557
1895	213,312	98,828	23,808	211,309	100,108	19,515
1896	219,233	101,130	27,199	..	..	..
1897	229,382	103,838	34,381	217,332	105,860	24,632
1898	227,642	105,453	34,736	205,937	108,196	9,593
1899	223,737	106,547	24,620	210,643	107,343	10,693
1900	224,429	108,868	23,719	191,713	108,550	150
1901	200,747	113,195	523	179,880	113,084	185
1902	202,974	112,602	1,433	196,613	107,284	360
1903	202,518	112,982	342	200,038	121,691	332
1904	212,771	115,156	254	197,417	114,212	Nil.
1905	206,602	114,879	Nil.	203,509	144,076	Nil.
1906	221,055	166,912	Nil.	215,846	155,719	Nil.
1907	220,628	143,936	Nil.	224,464	156,069	Nil.
1908	247,900	154,829	Nil.	261,874	153,868	Nil.
1909	273,319	148,096	Nil.	279,611	152,673	Nil.
1910	300,046	143,331	31,027	300,806	150,593	28,271
1911	327,170	152,741	48,027	322,815	170,160	50,528
1912	344,255	140,952	48,527	346,655	149,109	50,730

The Northern Heights, the Widened Lines, and Ludgate Hill

By the early 1900s, the Great Northern Railway's suburban network was doing impressive business but, in the eyes of the company's customers, overcrowding and delays were becoming intolerable. Various suggestions were made for improving matters, and these included a strong lobby for the GNR to operate some trains non-stop between Holloway and Farringdon Street, while a further deputation requested that the company reduce the already cheaply-priced workmen's tickets between Enfield and Moorgate Street. The GNR appreciated that it could not ignore its public as, at that time, Charles Yerkes's intention of creating an 'underground' empire posed a serious threat of direct competition for the North London traffic. In 1903, the GNR considered electrifying its Northern Heights branches, but the outlay required resulted in the scheme being dropped. The GNR nevertheless did what it could to placate its critics, but it had to contend with the competition of a new electrified 'tube' line between Moorgate and Finsbury Park.

A further blow to the GNR was that the electrification of the Inner Circle resulted in a drop in passengers on the long-standing GNR cross-London services via the Widened Lines and Ludgate Hill, and these were consequently withdrawn on 1 October 1907. The Midland's services through Ludgate Hill ceased from 1 July 1908 thereby bringing an end to the last direct local passenger services between Ludgate Hill and Farringdon Street. The last regular 'foreign' passenger working at Ludgate Hill ended after World War 1 when the LSWR withdrew its services from there to Richmond via Brixton.

A combination of Henry Ivatt design work and Doncaster engineering resulted in the Great Northern Railway's extremely smart 'C2' (later LNER 'C12') class 4-4-2Ts. The first 10 members of the 60-strong class were intended for work in the West Riding of Yorkshire, but the other 50 were used to replace Stirling 0-4-4Ts on London suburban services. The class's basic dimensions, as listed by the LNER in 1923, were: 5ft 8in coupled wheels, 18in x 26in cylinders, 170lb boilers, 1,350gall tanks and weights of 34tons 10cwt; the tractive effort at 85% was 17,900lb. Condensing apparatus was fitted from new to all of the London area locomotives, but it was removed when they were later transferred to other areas. Admittedly, the location of this picture, Enfield, was never part of the Underground system, although the GNR considered the electrification of the Enfield line in 1903. The engine in the picture, GNR No 1504, was built in March 1899, became LNER No 4504 (later No 7362), and was withdrawn as BR No 67362 in January 1958, some of its last years having been spent allocated to Mexborough shed in Yorkshire. Note the revolving destination board above the locomotive's front buffer beam.
Ian Allan Library

Right:

The style of condensing pipes on GNR 4-4-2T No 1539 was different from those on classmate No 1504, the version worn here by No 1539 later being adopted as standard for all condenser-fitted GNR locomotives. This locomotive survived until April 1955, although its underground workings in London were by then very much a thing of the past. The picture was taken at High Barnet, which became part of the Underground network in 1940.
Bucknall Collection/Ian Allan Library

Centre right:

The GNR's 'now-it-opens-now-it-closes' branch to Alexandra Palace was a popular haunt for Ivatt's 4-4-2Ts, No 1505 displaying its original square-ended bunker at Crouch End on an 'Ally Pally' working. In the late 1930s, the branch was included in plans for the Northern Line 'tube' extension but, although conductor rails were actually laid, no electric trains ever ran on the line.
Bucknall Collection/Ian Allan Library

Great Northern Railway 4-4-2T No 1531 emerges from the south end of Copenhagen tunnel with a Moorgate-bound train in the early 1900s.
Bucknall Collection/Ian Allan Library

Below:

In February 1903 Henry Ivatt placed the order for 0-8-2T No 116 for the GNR. The master plan was for the mighty steed to work GNR freight trains over the Widened Lines, but its massive proportions caused the Metropolitan's Civil Engineer to ban it from working over Met tracks. Consequently, it was fitted with a smaller diameter boiler and shortened tanks, the modifications resulting in a 1¾-ton reduction in its axle weight. This fine picture shows it in its rebuilt condition *circa* 1910.

Ten 0-8-2Ts similar to the modified No 116 were built by the GNR in 1904 for heavy London suburban duties. Despite their remarkable acceleration, which enabled times on the Moorgate-High Barnet services to be cut by five minutes, they were still considered rather too cumbersome to be accommodated comfortably at Moorgate and were soon displaced by 0-6-2Ts. By the end of 1907 all the 0-8-2Ts (Nos 117-26 plus the class leader, No 116) had been transferred to Colwick, their condensing apparatus having been removed prior to their reallocation.
Bucknall Collection/Ian Allan Library

Bottom:

Stirling's final saddle tank design for the GNR was that of the 'J13' (later LNER 'J52') class. Designed primarily for assisting with the ever-increasing exchange traffic via the Widened Lines and Ludgate Hill, the 'J13s' first appeared in 1892. The second class member to be delivered was GNR No 922, later LNER No 3922 and, ultimately, BR No 68757. Evidence of the locomotive's transfer work is provided by the wagons and sheets, the letters 'LCDR' being somewhat conspicuous.
Bucknall Collection/Ian Allan Library

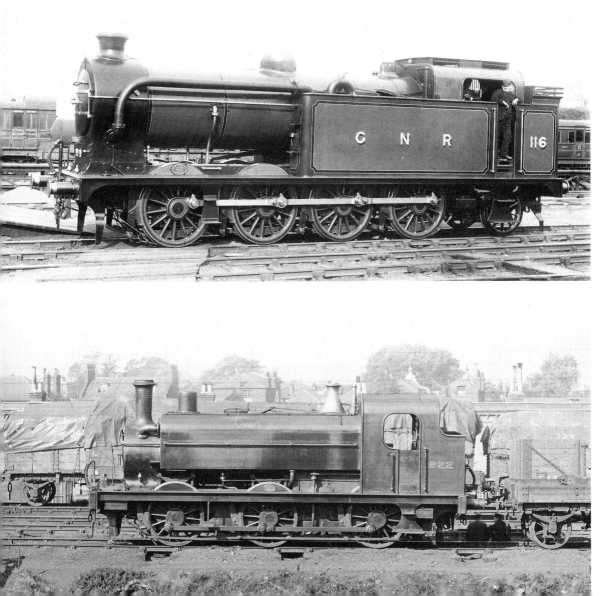

Left:
The Midland Railway's Beyer Peacock condensing 4-4-0Ts, Nos 204-209, were fitted with cabs in 1900/01. However, it was rather late in the day as all six were retired by the end of 1912, most of them having lost their condensing apparatus in their final years. This picture shows No 205 at Kentish Town around the turn of the century.
Ian Allan Library

Centre left:
The delightful 2-4-0Ts designed by Francis Webb and built for the LNWR in 1876-80 were all condenser-fitted for working on the Widened Lines. No 2247 was the penultimate member of the class to be retired. When it went to its grave as LMSR No 6425 in 1936 only No 6428 remained, but that stalwart hung on until 1952 when, as BR No 58092, it was withdrawn from duties on the Cromford & High Peak line. That was a far cry from working through the tunnels to Moorgate.
Ian Allan Library

Below:
The Midland's '2228' class 0-4-4Ts first appeared in 1895, the initial twenty being built by Dubs & Co; consequently, they carried that builder's distinctive diamond-shaped works plates. They had larger cylinders and tanks than their predecessors. Here, condenser-fitted No 2232 poses at Kentish Town shed.
Ian Allan Library

Above:

Francis Webb's 2-4-2Ts for the LNWR first appeared in 1879, 20 condenser-fitted members of the class being built in 1889/90. This is No 781 with a rake of LNWR teak coaches *circa* 1900; the destination board makes for interesting reading: 'Willesden Junction for North Western Main Line and Mansion House'.
Bucknall Collection/Ian Allan Library

Right:

The 'R' class 0-4-4Ts of the LC&DR were augmented by 15 slightly larger variants (designated 'R1s') after the 'merger' with the SER. One of the later batch was No 709, seen here with the obligatory condensing gear for cross-London workings.
Bucknall Collection/Ian Allan Library

Below right:

A remarkable total of 118 of James Stirling's 'Q' class 0-4-4Ts were built for the South Eastern Railway between 1881 and 1897, 55 of them being reboilered and reclassified 'Q1' by Harry Wainwright between 1903 and 1919. A distinctive feature of No 180 was the shortened chimney which enabled the engine to work to the Great Northern main line via Snow Hill and the Widened Lines.
Bucknall Collection/Ian Allan Library

Above:
GWR No 643, one of the condenser-fitted members of the '633' class 0-6-0Ts of 1871/72, was eventually fitted with a larger bunker but retained its open cab until its withdrawal in 1934.
Ian Allan Library

Below:
In the late 1890s, 30 of the GWR's 'Metro' class 2-4-0Ts were fitted with larger 1,080gall tanks, primarily to provide a greater capacity for subterranean workings in London. One was No 3562, built in 1894 and so converted in 1898.
Ian Allan Library

The West London Railway and the GWR lines

Even the West London Railway couldn't completely escape electrification. The first section was converted in 1906 although the many through workings remained steam-hauled. By the end of that year, electric services had taken over on the Hammersmith-Aldgate route but, until 1910, a GWR steam railmotor provided a half-hourly service between Ladbroke Grove and Richmond. From the start of 1911 the Great Western's passenger services to Aldgate were handled by Metropolitan electric locomotives, albeit with the exception of two daily steam workings.

The East London Railway

One of the few sections of the old network which remained exclusively steam-operated for a little longer was the East London Railway, but the reason for non-conversion to electric traction was hardly a case of traditionalism. The line was jointly leased and worked by the Metropolitan, the District, the London, Brighton & South Coast, the South Eastern & Chatham and the Great Eastern Railways, but when, in 1902, the Met and the District proposed electrification, the other lessees were unenthusiastic.

The ELR's route was a busy one, the 1902 figures showing that 276 passenger trains were accommodated every weekday, of which 100 were worked by the Met, 76 by the District, 64 by the LB&SCR and 36 by the GER. Furthermore, the ELR accommodated 32 GER-worked freight trains each day. Because the joint lessees of the ELR failed to back the electrification plans, the Met and the District withdrew their services on the line as from 3 December 1906, leaving the other users to carry on with steam-hauled workings for a few more years.

The period between the mid-1880s and the early 1900s was certainly a time of change for London's underground and inner suburban railways. Although the mass conversion to electric traction might have upset traditionalists, it made sound commercial sense and, of course, railway companies were in the business of making profits. By 1905 the Metropolitan alone carried over 95,000,000 passengers annually for receipts of over £1,000,000 and employed around 3,000 staff; the District Railway's figures for the same year showed receipts of some £410,000. Many higher-profile railway companies elsewhere in Britain must have looked enviously on those sorts of revenues.

It could be thought that the wearing of condensing apparatus in the middle of the Essex countryside was a little unnecessary, and the presence of an 'Epping' nameboard on a train at Brentwood Bank somewhat curious. However, this is a posed publicity picture showing 'G69' (later LNER 'F6') class 2-4-2T No 63 in a fully-lined royal blue livery, with a new varnished teak suburban set intended for Loughton and Epping services. Many years later, those services became part of the underground system.
Ian Allan Library

3
A change of emphasis

Despite the widespread and rapid electrification of London's underground and inner suburban railways in the early 1900s, steam traction was by no means completely eliminated. The Widened Lines route through to Moorgate Street was still ruled by steam, as was the cross-London line through Ludgate Hill, although the latter saw fewer and fewer through passenger workings. One of the very few new steam-worked lines which subsequently became part of the Underground map was the short branch from North Acton to Ealing. It was opened on 16 April 1917 and was initially used only by GWR goods trains, but a passenger service worked by the electric trains of the Central London Railway, one of the Underground's constituents, commenced in August 1920. However, despite the apparent unpromising prospect for steam workings on London's future Underground map, the heyday of steam-hauled operations on the Metropolitan Railway to the northwest of London had yet to come.

The addition of cabs to some of the Metropolitan's Beyer Peacock 4-4-0Ts might have been welcomed by engine crews, but they did not improve their engines' appearances. This is No 48, the penultimate member of the 'A' class to have been built. The introduction of the 'K' class 2-6-4Ts in 1924 resulted in the disposal of some of the remaining 'A' class 4-4-0Ts, No 7 being sold to the Mersey Railway, No 22 to the District Railway, and Nos 24/26/44 to Pelaw Main Colliery. *Bucknall Collection/Ian Allan Library*

The Metropolitan Railway

The Metropolitan's lines north of Harrow remained exclusively steam-worked until 1925, the company having formed, in April 1906, a joint committee with the Great Central to administer those lines. In 1908 the Metropolitan appointed Robert Hope Selbie as General Manager, part of his brief being to reverse the company's comparatively poor financial position after its massive outlay on electrification around Inner London. It was a difficult task, particularly as motorbuses offered additional competition for passenger revenue.

One of the areas which attracted Selbie's attention was the Baker Street-Aylesbury-Verney Junction route, much of which was already something of an up-market commuter line, and Selbie entered into negotiations with the Pullman Company for the provision of two suitably luxurious carriages for that route. The two cars, named *Galatea* and *Mayflower*, entered service on 1 June 1910 between Baker Street and Verney Junction; they were used singly with each one making five return trips each weekday, a supplement of 6d (2½p) being payable as far as Rickmansworth or 1s (5p) beyond. The Pullman cars were not particularly well patronised but, in terms of prestige and publicity, their value was immeasurable. Largely for those reasons, they were retained until October 1939.

In 1919, the Metropolitan transferred its unused building land to a specially-incorporated subsidiary, Metropolitan Railway Country Estates Ltd, and this sparked a major success story in the field of marketing. The new subsidiary promoted up-market housing developments in the outer suburbs of northwest London, the sales pitch being that journeys to and from work in Central London could be undertaken easily by the Metropolitan Railway. 'Metro-Land' was born, and it introduced business commuting on a vast scale. Naturally, the railway company benefited enormously.

Although the Metropolitan's image was that of a passenger carrier, the company certainly did not ignore freight. On the 'main line' to Aylesbury and Verney Junction every station but one beyond Northwood had freight facilities by 1904, most having been provided when the stations had first opened. Quainton Road became a busy interchange point and by 1927 up to 2,500 wagons were exchanged there each week. In 1914 the Met's stud of freight rolling stock comprised 362 low-sided wagons, 108 high-sided, and 24 box vans, the emphasis on opens being due to the main inwards traffic consisting of coal; coke from the gasworks at South Harrow, Pinner, Rickmansworth and Aylesbury provided much of the outwards traffic. The vans were used largely for transporting bulk foodstuffs from London Docks to a wholesaler's warehouse at Uxbridge.

Parcels traffic contributed a respectable amount to the Met's coffers, and during the Selbie regime the number of parcels handled annually by the company virtually doubled to almost 800,000. The building boom inspired by the 'Metro-Land' promotion in the 1920s and 1930s resulted in a considerable quantity of construction materials being transported by the Met, and substantial new siding accommodation had to be provided at Neasden, Hillingdon and Rayners

Right:
The Metropolitan Railway issued a leaflet 'Metro Cheap Fares to London' in November 1930. The prices make for very interesting reading.
Author's Collection

Below:
The Metropolitan Railway's accounts for 1913, as given in *Bradshaw's Shareholders' Guide.*

METROPOLITAN.		237
RECEIPTS AND EXPENDITURE.		
Subjoined are details for the year ended 31st December, 1913:—		
Receipts.	£	£
Passengers, parcels, &c.	688,690	
Merchandise, live stock, minerals, &c.	81,051	
Joint lines (Abstract J)	138,840	
Miscellaneous	5,726	
Rents	81,638	
Rents from leased lines	64,000	
Transfer fees	501	
Joint lines, Company's proportion of receipts other than in respect of railway working	30,302	
Amount receivable from Surplus Lands Committee	72,625	
	1,163,373	1,163,373
Expenses.		
Maintenance of way and works	46,453	
Do. rolling stock	69,955	
Locomotive running expenses	127,064	
Traffic expenses	131,790	
General charges	41,394	
Law charges and Parliamentary expenses	2,811	
Compensation (accidents and losses)	3,874	
Rates, taxes, and Government duty	39,057	
National Insurance Act, 1911. Health and unemployment	2,049	
Running powers	Cr. 34,328	
Total traffic expenditure	430,119	
Mileage, demurrage, &c.	1,255	
Miscellaneous	2,100	
Joint lines (Abstract J)	89,436	
Ordinary working expenses	522,910	
Interests, Rentals, and other fixed charges.		
Interest on debenture stocks	182,719	
Joint lines (Abstract J)	26,624	
Chief rents, wayleaves, General Renewals Fund and sundries (net)	43,218	
Dividend on preference stocks	211,482	
	986,953	986,953
Net balance		176,420
Balance brought from previous half-year		9,497
		185,917
Dividends on ordinary stock at 1½ per cent.		105,034
		80,883
Dividend on surplus lands stock at 2½ per cent.		72,625
Carried forward		£8,258

THIRD CLASS RETURN FARES TO

Upper table column headers (station destinations):
NORTHWICK PARK & KENTON, PRESTON ROAD, WEMBLEY PARK, NEASDEN & KINGSBURY, DOLLIS HILL, WILLESDEN GREEN & CRICKLEWOOD, KILBURN & BRONDESBURY, WEST HAMPSTEAD, FINCHLEY ROAD, SWISS COTTAGE, MARLBORO' ROAD, ST. JOHN'S WOOD, BAKER STREET, GREAT PORTLAND STREET, EUSTON SQUARE, KING'S CROSS & ST. PANCRAS, FARRINGDON & HIGH STREET, ALDERSGATE & BARBICAN, OLD STREET, ... MOORGATE STREET, ... BISHOPSGATE, ... LIVERPOOL STREET, ... MARK LANE, ... MANSION HOUSE, ALDGATE

FROM	Days on which Cheap Tickets are issued
*Verney Junction	
*Winslow Road	
*Granboro' Road	
*Brill	
*Wood Siding	
*Wotton	
*Westcott	Thursdays, Saturdays, and Sundays.
*Waddesdon Road	
*Quainton Road	
*Waddesdon	
*Aylesbury	
Stoke Mandeville	
Wendover	
*Great Missenden	
Amersham & Chesham Bois	
Chesham	
∆Chalfont & Latimer	
∆Chorley Wood & Chenies	
Rickmansworth	
Watford	
Croxley Green	
Moor Park & Sandy Lodge	
Northwood	
Pinner	
North Harrow	Wednesdays, Saturdays, and Sundays.
Harrow-on-the-Hill	
oUxbridge	
oHillingdon	
Ickenham	
Ruislip	
‡Ruislip Manor	
Eastcote	
Rayners Lane (for Harrow Garden Village)	
West Harrow	
Northwick Park & Kenton	

Lower table column headers (station destinations):
ALDGATE EAST, ST. MARY'S WHITECHAPEL RD., SHADWELL, WAPPING, ROTHERHITHE, SURREY DOCKS, NEW CROSS & NEW CROSS GATE, MARK LANE, MONUMENT, CANNON STREET, EDGWARE ROAD, PADDINGTON, BAYSWATER, NOTTING HILL GATE, HIGH STREET KENSINGTON, GLOUCESTER ROAD, SOUTH KENSINGTON, ROYAL OAK, WESTBOURNE PARK, LADBROKE GROVE, LATIMER ROAD, WOOD LANE, SHEPHERD'S BUSH, ADDISON ROAD, HAMMERSMITH, ... , ... , ... , ADDISON ROAD

FROM	Days on which Cheap Tickets are issued
*Verney Junction	
*Winslow Road	
*Granboro' Road	
*Brill	
*Wood Siding	
*Wotton	
*Westcott	Thursdays, Saturdays, and Sundays.
*Waddesdon Road	
*Quainton Road	
*Waddesdon	
Aylesbury	
Stoke Mandeville	
‡Wendover	
‡Great Missenden	
Amersham & Chesham Bois	
Chesham	
∆Chalfont & Latimer	
∆Chorley Wood & Chenies	
Rickmansworth	
Watford	
Croxley Green	
Moor Park & Sandy Lodge	
Northwood	
Pinner	
North Harrow	Wednesdays, Saturdays, and Sundays.
Harrow-on-the-Hill	
oUxbridge	
oHillingdon	
Ickenham	
Ruislip	
‡Ruislip Manor	
Eastcote	
Rayners Lane (for Harrow Garden Village)	
West Harrow	
Northwick Park & Kenton	

AVAILABILITY OF TICKETS.

WEDNESDAYS, THURSDAYS and SATURDAYS By all trains after 10.0 a.m.   SUNDAYS By all trains.

Return on day of issue By any train.

∆ Passengers may also travel by the 9.45 a.m. train from Chalfont & Latimer.

* Passengers may also travel by the 8.50 a.m. train ex Verney Junction.   ∆ Passengers may also travel by the 9.52 a.m. train ex Chalfont & Latimer.   ‡ Passengers should ...
‡ Wood Lane Station is only open on special occasions and on nights when Greyhound Racing takes place at the White City.   Passengers ...
‡ Ruislip Manor Station is open between 10.0 a.m. and 6.0 p.m. on SUNDAY.

First Class Cheap Tickets at the approximate Single fare for the Return Journey are also issued between the above stations and on the same days.

CONDITIONS OF ISSUE OF TICKETS.

These tickets are issued subject to the Conditions of Issue of Ordinary Passenger Tickets, where applicable, and also to the following conditions.
Neither the holder nor any other person shall have any right of action against the Company or any other Railway Company or persons owning, working, or using any railway or ...
or premises (whether jointly with the Company or otherwise) open which such tickets may be available in respect of (a) injury (fatal or otherwise), loss, damage, or delay however caused, or (b) loss of or damage or delay to property however caused.
The tickets are available only by the trains and on the days specified in the Company's notices.
A ticket which covers the outward and return journey shall not be available for the return journey unless and until the outward journey has been completed.
If a ticket is used in contravention of these conditions, the holder will be required to pay the difference between the sum actually paid for the ticket and the full ordinary return fare between the stations named on such ticket.

BAKER STREET STATION, N.W.1.   CHILDREN UNDER 3 YEARS OF AGE FREE; 3 YEARS AND UNDER 14 YEARS HALF THE ABOVE FARES.   BY ORDER.

49

Lane. Most classes of the Met's freight traffic were handled at the impressive City Goods Depot at Vine Street which had opened in November 1909, but the trains between the depot and West Hampstead Yard were hauled exclusively by electric locomotives.

When the grouping of Britain's railways was under discussion after World War 1, there were suggestions that one of the proposed groups should include all the railways operating suburban services in the London area but, as the history books show, the 'London Group' was not to be. Instead, the Metropolitan was excluded completely from the Grouping and, during the 1920s and the early 1930s, the Met delivered an object lesson in the efficient running of a commuter service. For the steam enthusiasts of the day, however, the extension of electrification to Rickmansworth in January 1925 took away a little of the gloss.

Just to the east, the branch to Watford opened on 2 November 1925 with services being provided by both the Metropolitan and the LNER. Ironically, though, the LMSR services between nearby Watford Junction and Euston were, on average, some 10 minutes faster than the Met's electric Watford-Baker Street services. As for the LNER's steam-hauled Watford-Marylebone workings, they were poorly patronised and, after temporary suspension during the General Strike of 1926, were not reinstated on a regular basis.

Towards the Metropolitan's extremity, Aylesbury station was largely reconstructed in 1926 with two platforms, each of 665ft length, and a 545ft bay for London trains. Along the line at Quainton Road, operations on the anachronistic Brill branch continued their leisurely existence, with veteran Metropolitan 4-4-0Ts in charge of proceedings until 1 December 1935, when the branch's average annual loss of £4,000 during the preceding years was finally considered enough to warrant total closure. Furthermore, passenger services were finally withdrawn between Quainton Road and Verney Junction on 4 July 1936.

Above right:
One of the Met's remaining Beyer Peacock '4-4-0Ts hauls what appears to be a permanent way train near Harrow-on-the-Hill in the mid-1930s. The main line was quadrupled as far as Harrow in 1932, quadrupling beyond there not being completed until after the war.
Ian Allan Library

Right:
Metropolitan 'E' class 0-4-4T No 82 was one of the four members of the class to be withdrawn shortly after the birth of the London Passenger Transport Board in 1933.
Ian Allan Library

Above:
Metropolitan 'E' class 0-4-4T No 80 was photographed at Chesham in June 1934. The locomotive subsequently became No L47 in London Transport stock.
Rail Archive Stephenson

Left:
An unidentified 'F' class 0-4-4T is seen hauling the breakdown train away from Neasden depot.
Bucknall Collection/Ian Allan Library

Below left:
Metropolitan 'F' class 0-6-2T No 93 was photographed near Rickmansworth with a ballast train *circa* 1920.
Bucknall Collection/Ian Allan Library

Below:
The design of the Metropolitan's 'G' class 0-6-4Ts was accredited to Charles Jones, the company's Chief Mechanical Engineer, although many of the locomotives' features smacked strongly of the Great Central. The 'Gs' were the first Met engines to be superheated, Robinson (GCR)-style superheaters being fitted from new.

Although initially intended for mixed traffic duties, the 'Gs' spent much of their later lives on freight workings. The four members of the class, Nos 94-97, were built by the Yorkshire Engine Co in 1915/16 and had 5ft 9in diameter coupled wheels, 20in x 26in cylinders, 160lb boilers, grate areas of 21.4 sqft, and weighed in at 71tons 7cwt apiece. Their nominal tractive effort was 20,498lb. The locomotives were named as follows: 94 *Lord Aberconway,* 95 *Robert H. Selbie*, 96 *Charles Jones* and 97 *Brill*

The Met's decision to name the 'G' class 0-6-4Ts caused considerable surprise, although the naming of Nos 94/95 after the company's Chairman and General Manager respectively was perfectly orthodox practice. However, the names applied to Nos 96/97 caused many an eyebrow to be raised once again. In the case of No 96, it was extremely rare for any company to name a locomotive after its designer prior to his retirement. As for No 97, Brill was the terminus of the lightly-laid and extremely rural branch from Quainton Road. Not only did Brill fail to typify the general sphere of operations of the Metropolitan Railway, but the locomotive which carried the name was too heavy to work on the branch. The choice of name for No 97 was most curious.

All four 'G' class 0-6-4Ts outlived the Metropolitan Railway itself. On 1 November 1937 all steam workings north of Rickmansworth were transferred to the LNER, and so were 18 ex-Metropolitan steam locomotives. Among them were the 'Gs', which became LNER 'M2' class Nos 6154-57. No 6157 (ex-Met No 97) was withdrawn in 1943 and No 6154 (ex-No 94) in 1946, the other two being renumbered 9076/77 in 1946/47. Although designated BR Nos 69076/77 at Nationalisation, the two survivors were retired in October 1948 without having carried their allotted numbers. This picture shows No 97 *Brill* at Neasden in 1932.
Bucknall Collection/Ian Allan Library

Right:
During the 1920s and 1930s the use of 'G' class 0-6-4Ts on passenger workings was not particularly common. Nevertheless, No 94 *Lord Aberconway* was photographed at Rickmansworth in 1937 after bringing in a train from Aylesbury. The locomotive is seen leaving its train so that an electric locomotive can take over for the rest of the journey to Baker Street. *C. R. L. Coles*

Eight 'H' class superheated 4-4-4Ts were built by Kerr Stuart in 1920/21 to a design of Charles Jones, the Metropolitan's CME, although, like the 'G' class 0-6-4Ts, there was ample evidence of Great Central influence in the design work. The 'Hs' had 5ft 9in driving wheels, 19in x 26in cylinders, grate areas of 21.4 sqft and 160lb boilers; they weighed 78tons 5cwt and had a nominal tractive effort of 18,500lb. The 'Hs' were intended for the Met's fastest passenger services. Their introduction enabled some Baker Street-Aylesbury trains (which were usually loaded to 250 tons) to be accelerated to 43min, including the locomotive change at Wembley Park. In the speed stakes, they were regularly known to reach 75mph on the descent of Chorley Wood bank. The emergence of the 'Hs' resulted in not only the 'G' class 0-6-4Ts being displaced from regular passenger work, but also the subsequent retirement of the two remaining 'C' class 0-4-4Ts and the six 'D' class 2-4-0Ts.

The 'Hs' were very smart-looking engines and, predictably, were regarded as the 'flagships' of the Metropolitan's fleet. All eight became LNER stock in 1937 and were designated the 'H2' class with numbers 6415-22. In 1941 they had their working boiler pressure raised to 170lb which resulted in an increased tractive effort of 19,656lb. At the end of that same year all eight were transferred from Neasden to Colwick shed in Nottingham, where they were put to work on local suburban services. Three of the class subsequently had short stays at Langwith, but in stark contrast to their reputations at Neasden, the locomotives were unpopular with the crews at both Colwick and Langwith. All eight were withdrawn between 1942 and 1947, ex-Met Nos 104/05 (LNER Nos 6416/17) having become Nos 7511/12 in the LNER's renumbering scheme of 1946.

The style of lettering applied to No 104 in this picture was relatively short-lived and, furthermore, not consistently applied. It was in use from around 1910, and so this picture must have been taken when the locomotive was virtually brand-new.
Bucknall Collection/Ian Allan Library

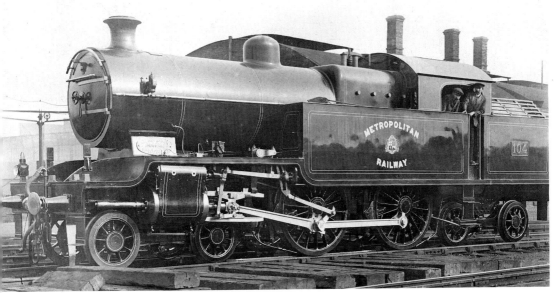

Left:
Metropolitan 'H' class 4-4-4T No 103, built by Kerr Stuart in 1920.
Bucknall Collection/Ian Allan Library

Above:
'H' class 4-4-4T No 105 shows off its mid-1930s livery. Despite the locomotive's impressive proportions, the blatant lack of spit and polish makes for a sad comparison with classmate No 104 in the earlier picture.
Ian Allan Library

Left:
This Aylesbury working of the early 1920s was photographed north of Rickmansworth, 'H' class 4-4-4T No 103 being in charge.
Ian Allan Library

Below left:
'K' class 2-6-4T No 112 is seen on a freight working near Amersham *circa* 1932.
Ian Allan Library

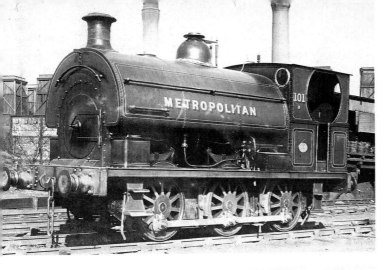

Left:
The Metropolitan's Peckett 0-4-0ST No 101 was photographed at Neasden in the early 1930s. When taken into London Transport stock, No 101 and its classmate, No 102, became Departmental Nos L53/54, and the latter survived until September 1961.
Ian Allan Library

Centre left:
Verney Junction was the extremity of the Metropolitan Railway's system. In May 1936, a little over two months before the withdrawal of passenger services between Quainton Road and Verney Junction, 'H' class 4-4-4T No 107 waits with a Quainton Road train. The train disappearing on the left hand side of the picture is on the ex-LNWR line to Bletchley.
H. C. Casserley

Bottom left:
The Brill branch was closed on 1 December 1935. It was a total contrast to the more familiar parts of the Metropolitan's system, as evidenced by this 'classic country branch' scene. During the branch's final years, Beyer Peacock 4-4-0Ts Nos 23 and 41 were the regular engines, each doing a week at a time on the branch; the former is seen at Wood Siding in the summer of 1935. No 41 was scrapped in 1936, but its classmate, No 23, was renumbered in London Transport stock as No L45 and soldiered on until 1948, when it was withdrawn for preservation and subsequently restored to its original cabless condition.
Ian Allan Library

The Widened Lines

Apart from the Metropolitan Railway, the companies most involved with suburban passenger services in northern London were, arguably, the North London Railway and the Great Northern Railway. The story of the former, although fascinating, is outside the scope of this book, but the latter had forged strong links with the Metropolitan Railway from the very beginning of underground workings in London.

The GNR saw a continuing increase in suburban traffic from its own catchment area, many services terminating not at King's Cross but at Moorgate Street which, in October 1924, had its name formally abbreviated to Moorgate. The final stage of the journey to Moorgate was via the Widened Lines and, although the locomotives designated for that duty were fitted with condensing gear, many drivers chose not to use the apparatus. The general attitude was that, as the condensers warmed the water in the tanks, the operation of the boiler injectors became unreliable and, furthermore, the minimal exhaust draught severely reduced a locomotive's steaming abilities. On Widened Lines turns, good time-keeping was essential to avoid delaying the numerous other workings, and so it was usually considered that the use of the condensing equipment, with the resultant reduction in power, would cause more problems than it solved.

The junction where the GNR/LNER trains joined the Widened Lines almost under King's Cross was controlled by a small gas-lit signalbox 28ft below street level and, although official access to the box was by means of a manhole in the road, signalmen normally preferred the hazardous walk alongside the tracks through the tunnel. The lack of visibility in the smoky cavern was evidenced by the fact that it was not unknown for trains to be wrongly identified by signalmen, more than one Midland/LMS train being routed to the surface at King's Cross by mistake.

Ivatt's 'N1' class 0-6-2Ts for the Great Northern Railway were intended to take over some of the heavier suburban work in the London area. A total of 56 'N1s' were built between 1907 and 1912, all but four being fitted with condensing apparatus from new. GNR No 1601 was one of the last to be built and is seen at High Barnet on 18 May 1923 with confirmation of its post-Grouping ownership, but nevertheless retaining its GNR number. The locomotive became LNER No 4601, that number being applied in 1925; it became No 9481 under the 1946 renumbering scheme and, after Nationalisation, became BR No 69481. By then, it still lived at King's Cross shed, but was later transferred to Yorkshire, prior to which it had its condensing apparatus removed.

The sight of 0-6-2Ts, albeit often 'N2s', at High Barnet continued for about a year after the commencement of Northern Line electric services on 14 April 1940. While the electrification of the High Barnet line might have been a disappointment for steam enthusiasts, London Transport was delighted at the increase in traffic. Some 3.5 million passengers used the line in the steam-worked year of 1934 but by 1947 the figure was 12 million.
Lens of Sutton

Right:
The Great Eastern's 'L77' (later LNER 'N7') class 0-6-2Ts were altogether different from the GNR's 'N1' 0-6-2Ts. The GER's 0-6-2Ts were designed by Alfred Hill, the first two being built at Stratford early in 1915. That initial pair consisted of one superheated engine and one saturated, the idea being to compare the two before embarking on a production series.

It took a little while for that production series to materialise, ten engines being built in the last half of 1921. Nevertheless, the LNER was suitably impressed by the fast acceleration shown by the engines, and a total of 122 more were built between 1923 and 1928. One of the 1925 batch was LNER No 916, which survived until 1959 as BR No 69655.
Ian Allan Library

Centre right:
The 1935 scheme for extending electric 'tube' services throughout the Northern Heights included the Alexandra Palace branch but, despite considerable preparatory work, the branch was never electrified. During the years of austerity which followed World War 2, traffic figures on the branch declined considerably. Passenger services were ultimately withdrawn on 5 July 1954 although the occasional goods trains worked to Muswell Hill until 14 June 1956 and to Cranley Gardens until 18 May 1957. This picture, therefore, is a 'what might have been'.

As an interim measure before the proposed electrification of the Alexandra Palace branch, push-pull services were introduced on 7 September 1942. Ex-GCR 'F2' class 2-4-2Ts monopolised branch duties until the class's extinction in 1950, former GNR 'C12' class 4-4-2Ts taking over until the cessation of the branch's passenger services. This late-1940s picture of an 'Ally Pally' working shows 'F2' No 7108 which was retired in July 1950 without having carried its designated BR number of 67108.
P. Ransome Wallis

Left:
The Midland Railway's Kirtley-designed 0-4-4WTs of 1870 were condenser-fitted from new. No 1224 survived until 1928, but some of its contemporaries hung on for around seven more years. The shedplate (16) is that of the locomotive's home depot, Kentish Town.
Ian Allan Library

The West London Railway

Steam retained a distinct presence on the West London Railway despite the introduction of the Addison Road-Aldgate electric service in 1906. The tenacity of steam traction on the WLR was due largely to the line's importance as a connecting route, seven different companies being serviced along its six route miles. The variety of services using the WLR was vast and included, between July 1906 and June 1907, a fast LB&SCR Brighton-Paddington working, usually hauled throughout by Marsh 'I1' class 4-4-2Ts or Billinton 'B4' class 4-4-0s.

Among the through carriages accommodated on the WLR line, the best known were those of the 'Sunny South Special', a Liverpool-Brighton-Eastbourne service which was introduced in July 1904. The northern part of the 'Sunny South's' journey was later operated by the LNWR as a separate train, LB&SCR engines taking over at Willesden, and over the years it was augmented with through coaches between Liverpool and Dover, Manchester and Deal, and others for Margate and Ramsgate. The 'Sunny South' continued operating until 1939, but two other through workings over the WLR had shorter lives. A Liverpool-Weymouth and a Liverpool-Dover service were both inaugurated in 1905, but the former was discontinued in 1910 and the latter in 1915. In later years, a Saturdays Only Coventry-Bournemouth service traversed the WLR, that being introduced in 1929 but ceasing in 1933.

By 1920 the suburban passenger trains using Kensington (Addison Road) station had fallen in number to around 80 each weekday, ie well under half the number of 35 years earlier. Among the more local turns over the WLR, the GWR, for example, worked a Victoria-Southall service and used steam railmotors between Clapham Junction (occasionally Victoria) and Greenford. The Willesden Junction-Earls Court services of the LNWR were given over to electric traction on 1 May 1914, District Railway rolling stock being used until the LNWR's own stock was delivered in November. On the WLR line, the station at Kensington (Addison Road) was officially suffixed 'for Olympia' in 1924 in recognition of the increasing popularity of the exhibition hall, the more familiar name of Olympia not being applied until December 1946.

Right:
The LSWR working timetable for 1 June to 30 September 1909 detailed the passenger services between Kensington (Addison Road) and Clapham Junction on the old West London Railway.

Left:
The route of the old West London Extension Railway continued to accommodate steam-hauled workings right through to the 1960s. For many years a remarkable variety of locomotives were seen on the line, sections of which once hosted Metropolitan and District Railway trains. The most celebrated passenger working along the line was the 'Sunny South Express', the second part of which was hauled, on 26 August 1933, by SR 'U1' class 2-6-0 No 1905. The location is Kensington (Addison Road) station.
H. C. Casserley

Below left:
A push-pull sandwich enters Kensington (Addison Road) on 26 August 1933. The locomotive is ex-LNWR Webb 'Coal Tank' No 7710.
H. C. Casserley

WEST LONDON EXTENSION LINE.

FOR SPEED RESTRICTIONS SEE PAGES A, B, C and D.

DOWN TRAINS.—WEEK DAYS

Note.—Trains marked S are South Western Trains, and run to and from the South Western Platforms at Clapham Junction, and Trains marked B are Brighton Company's Trains, and those marked NW are L.& N.W. Company's, and both run to and from Brighton Company's Platforms at Clapham Junction.

Distance. M. C.	STATIONS.	S.	S.	S.	S. Ety.	B.	B.	S.	B.	B	S	B	S.	S.	B.	S.	NW	S.	S.W. Horse Box Train Wimbledon. arr. dep. a.m. a.m.	B.	S	NW
		a.m.	a.m.	a.m.	a.m.	a.m.	a.m.	a.m.	a.m.	a.m.	a.m.	a.m.	a.m.	a.m.	a.m.	a.m.	a.m.	a.m.		p.m.	p.m.	p.m.
— —	**Clapham Jc.** (L.& S.W.)...dep.	5 39	6 5	6 35	6 45	...	...	7 42	...	...	8 51	...	9 20	9 48	...	1052	...	1152	11 55	...	1247	...	...
— 50	Do. (L.B.& S.C.) ,,	...	...	...	...	6 52	7 33	...	8 20	8 41	...	9 15	...	...	1010	...	1111	1138	...	...	1220	1 2	...
— 64	Latchmere Junc. pass	5 41	6 7	6 37	6 46	6 54	7 35	7 45	8 23	8 43	8 53	9 17	9 20	9 51	1015	1054	1113	1139	1154	...	1222	1249	1 4
1 58	Battersea ....dep.	5 42	6 8	6 38	6 47	6 55	7 36	7 45	8 23	8 44	8 54	9 18	9 23	9 51	1013	1055	1114	1141	1155	11 58	1223	1250	1 5
2 23	Chelsea & Fulham ,,	5 45	6 11	6 41	6 49	6 58	7 39	7 48	8 26	8 47	8 57	9 21	9 26	9 54	1016	1058	1117	1144	1158	12 1	1226	1253	1 8
3 25	West Brompton ... ,,	5 47	6 13	6 43	6 51	7 0	7 41	7 50	8 28	8 49	8 59	9 23	9 28	9 56	1018	11 0	1119	1146	12 0	12 3	1228	1255	1 10
	Kensington (Addison Road) arr.	5 50	6 16	6 46	6 53	7 3	7 44	7 53	8 31	8 52	9 2	9 26	9 31	9 59	1021	11 3	1122	1149	12 3	12 6	...	1231	1258	1 13

DOWN TRAINS.—WEEK DAYS.—Continued.

STATIONS.	B.	S.	B. †	S.	B.	B	S.	B.	S.	NW	B.	S.	B.	NW	S	B.	S.	B.	NW	S.	B	S Horse Boxes when required	S.	B	B	S
	p.m.	p.m.	p.m.	p.m.	p.m.	p.m.	p.m.	p.m.	p.m.	p.m.	p.m.	p.m.	p.m.	p.m.	p.m.	p.m.	p.m.	p.m.	p.m.	pm	p.m.	p.m.	pm	p.m.	p.m.	p.m.
Clapham Jc. (L.& S.W.)...dep.	...	1 8	...	1 53	...	...	3 48	...	4 43	...	...	5 30	...	...	6 44	...	7 40	...	...	8 45	...	9 35	951	...	10 8	1045
Do. (L.B.& S.C.) ,,	1 15	...	1 46	...	2 26	3 10	...	4 12	...	5 3	5 15	...	6 12	6 28	...	7 15	...	8 15	8 36	...	916	...	10 8	...	...	...
Latchmere Junc. pass	1 17	1 10	...	1 55	2 28	3 12	3 50	4 14	4 45	5 6	5 17	5 32	6 14	6 30	6 46	7 17	7 42	8 17	8 38	8 47	918	...	953	1010	1047	1119
Battersea ....dep.	1 18	...	1 55	2 29	3 13	3 51	4 14	4 46	5 7	5 18	5 33	6 15	6 31	6 47	7 18	7 43	8 18	8 39	8 48	919	...	954	1011	1048	1120
Chelsea & Fulham ,,	1 21	...	1 59	2 32	3 16	3 54	4 18	4 49	5 10	5 21	5 36	6 18	6 36	6 50	7 21	7 46	8 21	8 32	8 51	922	...	957	1014	1051	1123
West Brompton... ,,	1 23	...	2 1	2 34	3 18	3 56	4 20	4 51	5 13	5 23	5 38	6 20	6 39	6 52	7 23	7 48	8 23	8 34	8 53	924	...	959	1016	1053	1125
Kensington (Addison Road) arr.	1 26	1 16	2 4	2 37	3 21	3 59	4 23	4 54	5 16	5 26	5 41	6 23	6 42	6 55	7 26	7 51	8 26	8 37	8 56	927	9 47	102	1019	1056	1128

† Calls at Clapham Junction for working purposes only.

UP TRAINS.—WEEK DAYS.

Note.—Trains marked S are South Western Trains, and run to and from the South Western Platforms at Clapham Junction, and Trains marked B are Brighton Company's Trains, and those marked NW are L.& N.W. Company's, and both run to and from the Brighton Company's Platforms at Clapham Junction.

Distance. M. C.	STATIONS.	GW Mlk	S.	S.	S.	B.	B.	S	N.W. when required Sats.	B.	S.	B	B	NW	S.	B.	S.	NW	B.	S.	S.W. Horse Box Train Wimbledon. arr. dep. p.m. p.m.	B.	B. Sats. only.
		a.m.	a.m.	a.m.	a.m.	a.m.	a.m.	a.m.	a.m.	a.m.	a.m.	a.m.	a.m.	a.m.	a.m.	a.m.	a.m.	a.m.	a.m.	p.m.		p.m.	p.m.
— —	**Kensington** (Addison Road)...dep.	1 35	6 9	635	657	715	750	8 9	8 33	840	910	917	9 33	9 53	1016	1040	1110	1116	1140	1212	...	12 20	1240	1 16
1 2	West Brompton ...... ,,		612	638	7 0	718	753	812		843	913	920	9 36	9 56	1019	1043	1113	1119	1143	1215	12 23	1243	...
1 47	Chelsea & Fulham ... ,,		614	640	7 2	720	755	814		845	915	922	9 38	9 58	1021	1045	1116	1121	1145	1217	12 25	1245	...
2 42	Battersea .... ,,		617	643	7 5	723	758	817		848	918	925	9 41	10 1	1024	1048	1118	1124	1148	1220	12 28	1248	...
2 55	Latchmere Junc. pass		619	644	7 6	724	759	818		849	919	926	9 42	10 2	1025	1049	1119	1125	1149	1221		1249	...
3 25	**Clapham Jnc.** (L.B.& S.C.) arr.	1 45	...	...	...	726	8 1	...		854	...	928	9 44	10 4	...	1051	...	1127	1151	...		1251	1 25
— —	Do. (L.& S.W.) ,,		620	646	7 8	...	820	8 33	8 41	...	921	...	...	1027	...	1121	...	...	1223	12 30	12 36	...	...

UP TRAINS.—WEEK DAYS—Continued.

STATIONS.	S.	B	NW	S.	B	S	S Horse Box Train †	B	B.	S.	NW	B.	S	B.	S.	B.	NW	S.	S.	B.	S.	B.	S Horse Boxes when required	S.	B	B.	S	S
	p.m.	p.m.	p.m.	p.m.	p.m.	p.m.	p.m.	p.m.	p.m.	p.m.	p.m.	p.m.	p.m.	p.m.	p.m.	p.m.	p.m.	p.m.	p.m.	p.m.	pm	pm	p.m.	p.m.	p.m.	p.m.	p.m.	p.m.
Kensington (Addison Road) dep.	126	1 50	224	237	251	3 4	3 7	3 35	343	8 4	4 27	445	5 5	545	610	635	6 53	717	745	8 5	850	925	943	9 55	1010	1040	11 6	1125	1135
West Brompton ... ,,	129	153	227	240	254		...	346	4 41	4 30	448	548	613	638	6 56	720	748	8 8	853	928	946		1013	1043	11 9	1128	1138
Chelsea & Fulham ,,	131	155	229	242	256	3 8		348	4 4	4 32	450	510	550	615	640	6 58	722	750	810	855	930	948		1015	1045	1111	1130	1140
Battersea .... ,,	134	158	232	245	259		...	351	4 6	4 35	453	513	553	618	643	7 1	745	753	813	855	933	951		1018	1048	1114	1133	1143
Latchmere Junc. pass	135	159	233	246	3 0	3 10		352	417	4 36	454	514	554	619	644	7 2	7 36	754	814	859	934	952		1019	1050	1115	1134	1144
Clapham Jnc. (L.B.& S.C.) arr.	...	2 1	235	...	3 12		3†43	354	...	4 38	456	...	556	...	646	7 4	...	756	...	9 1	...	955		...	1051	1117	...	...
Do. (L.& S.W.) ,,	137	...	...	248	...	3 12	3 15	...	419	...	...	516	...	621	...	728	...	816	...	936	...	10 7		1021	...	...	1138	1147

† Calls at Clapham Junction for working purposes only.

Above:

A southbound cross-London freight trundles through Addison Road on 26 August 1933 behind LMSR-built '7F' 0-8-0 No 9507.

H. C. Casserley

Below:

The station at West Brompton on the old West London Extension Railway was alongside that of the District Railway, but the former closed on 21 October 1940. Two GWR 0-6-0PTs, Nos 8700 and 5727, haul a northbound transfer freight through West Brompton on 28 August 1933. The leading locomotive, No 8700, was later renumbered as 9700, the first in a sequence of 11 condenser-fitted locomotives which more usually worked over the Widened Lines to Smithfield.

H. C. Casserley

Right:

Chelsea & Fulham station was the last WLER station on the north side of the Thames. On 28 August 1933, a little over seven years before the station closed, the 5.42pm Addison Road-Clapham Junction working was hauled by ex-LB&SCR 'D3' 0-4-4T No B398. The road over the railway at the far end of the station is Fulham Road.

H. C. Casserley

The East London Railway

The electrification of the East London Railway was not completed until 31 March 1913, the old engine and carriage sheds at New Cross (SER) subsequently being converted for use by the new EMUs. Just prior to the line's electrification it hosted 100 LB&SCR trains to and from Shoreditch each weekday, 98 SER trains to and from Whitechapel and 32 GER workings to and from Liverpool Street; in addition, there were 54 GER freight trains, many of which worked to or from Spitalfields. A little under two years before the electrification of the ELR, services had been even more numerous, the LB&SCR services to Old Kent Road and Peckham Rye, and the GER trains to Croydon, having operated until June 1911.

The working of the ELR was transferred from the old Joint Committee to the Metropolitan in 1921, but condenser-fitted GER 'R24' (later LNER 'J67') class 0-6-0Ts continued to work the freight trains through to Hither Green, New Cross Gate and Norwood Junction yard. Because of the 1 in 40 gradients on the approaches to the Thames Tunnel, the 0-6-0Ts' loadings were restricted to 22 wagons, a speed limit of 15mph prevailing. The ELR nominally became Southern Railway property in 1925 but, due to the complex nature of the long-standing joint lease, the Metropolitan, the District and the LNER each retained a 17½% interest.

World War 1 and after

During World War 1, the first major disruption of train services on the steam-operated 'underground' lines was on 7 July 1917 when an unexploded bomb at Moorgate Yard played havoc with scheduling. The following year, on the night of 28/29 January, the Widened Lines were blocked by debris from a bombed warehouse and normal services could not recommence for two days. Countless Londoners chose to move out of the city centre during the war, many of those heading for the northwestern outskirts travelling by the Metropolitan Railway. Because of the increased traffic, the Met eliminated the Harrow stop from a number of its workings and, instead, the changeover from electric to steam traction was made at Wembley Park. Although that alteration to normal working practice had been made from necessity, it proved very successful and was retained after the war, new track and signal arrangements being provided at Wembley Park in 1918.

To economise on coal consumption during the war years, the Met decelerated off-peak services but escaped with only a 12% cut in its total train mileage, a far lower reduction than had been imposed on some other companies. Conversely, the SE&CR cited the need for economies as a thinly-veiled excuse for withdrawing its passenger services into Moorgate Street as from 3 April 1916. Even before the war, a survey had revealed that on the 52 SE&CR trains arriving at Moorgate Street in a 24hr period, only 78 passengers had been carried. With the cessation of the SE&CR workings into Moorgate Street, the signalbox at the Smithfield Curve became redundant and control was later transferred to Aldersgate; furthermore, Holborn Viaduct (Low Level) station was also rendered superfluous and was formally closed on 1 June. The nearby station at Ludgate Hill had been extensively rebuilt in 1910, but even that didn't guarantee an indefinite life as it was closed on 3 March 1929.

The mass-mobilisation during the war resulted in intensive use of the Widened Lines by north-south troop trains, a peak of 58 in one day being reached when the British Expeditionary Force was on the move to France. By the end of the war it was calculated that 26,047 special mili-

Despite the electrification of most of London's underground railways, the Widened Lines remained a bastion of steam traction. In this superb picture of *circa* 1920 Midland Railway 0-4-4T No 1316 leaves Aldersgate with a train for East Ham. The locomotive was built at Derby in 1886 and was originally No 1723. It was fitted with condensing apparatus in 1889 and renumbered in 1907; it was withdrawn in 1925, but a few of its older classmates clung on until the 1950s.
Ian Allan Library

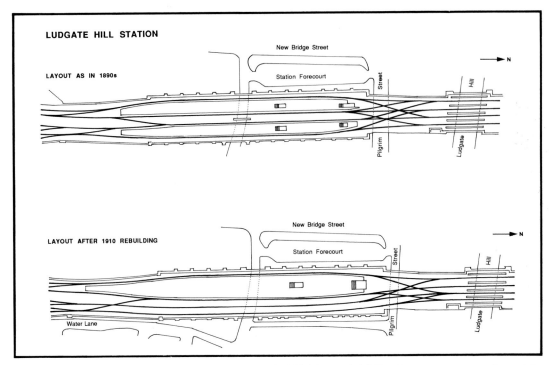

LUDGATE HILL STATION

LAYOUT AS IN 1890s

New Bridge Street

Station Forecourt

New Bridge Street

LAYOUT AFTER 1910 REBUILDING

Station Forecourt

Water Lane

The rebuilding of Ludgate Hill station in 1910 with less platform faces did little to ensure a lengthy life, as the station closed on 3 March 1929. The 1890s and 1910 layouts are shown for comparison.

tary workings had used the route. As for the additional freight workings, a remarkable total of 2,935 relief freight trains used the Widened Lines during the first two weeks of February 1915 alone, around ¼ million tons of freight being conveyed during the four years of hostilities. In order to help accommodate the extra traffic, the GNR, SE&CR and Midland passenger services into Farringdon Street were restricted to the rush hours, and facilities for a second banking engine were provided. In practice, however, the light-running of returning bankers did little to ease the congestion.

Things gradually returned to normal after the war, but the off-peak weekday services via the Widened Lines into Moorgate Street remained conspicuous by their absence although, on Saturdays, the station accommodated a fair number of workings throughout much of the day. At Moorgate the up road was electrified in 1926 to provide access for rush hour electric trains, but the live rails were taken out in 1935.

The Widened Lines joined the outside world at King's Cross. The climb up the Hotel Curve from the Widened Lines was usually guaranteed to provide the ubiquitous 'full head of steam' so beloved by railway photographers, but the comings and goings at the unsung end of King's Cross station were comparatively sparsely recorded. It seems that static Gresley Pacifics had more photographic appeal than hard-working 0-6-2Ts. In this late 1920s picture, 'N1' No 4583 (later BR No 69463) hauls a train of decidedly non-LNER wagons, having presumably worked from one of the South London yards via Snow Hill.

Lens of Sutton

Right:
An unidentified ex-SE&CR 'B1' 4-4-0 was photographed at Snow Hill (Holborn Viaduct, Low Level) on 4 April 1933, just over 15 years after the station had closed. For much of the short run between Holborn Viaduct and Farringdon, the railway was something of a 'now you see it, now you don't' affair which offered some truly atmospheric conditions for the few photographers who bothered to record it.

Brian Stephenson Collection

Left:
Evening sunshine was able to brighten at least part of the station at Aldersgate. Midland Railway 0-4-4T No 1380 (built in 1893 as No 2227) was photographed at Aldersgate *circa* 1921/22, and provides a contrast with the District Railway Circle Line train on the left.

Real Photographs

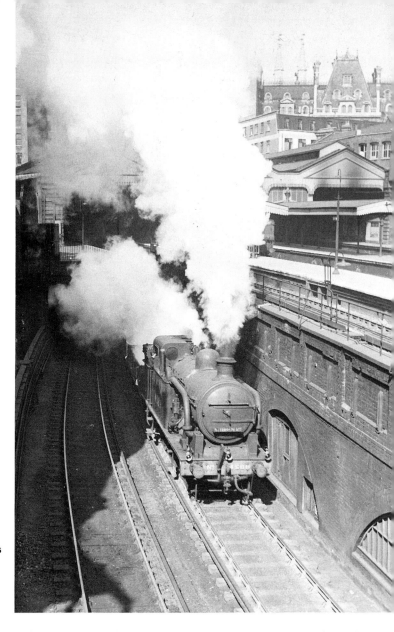

Right:
The 'Alexandra Palace' headboard on LNER 'N1' 0-6-2T No 4589 might have caused a little confusion to the public on 4 April 1933. The train is, in fact, a cross-London freight working which has travelled via part of the Widened Lines to emerge in the daylight alongside a very under-used Holborn Viaduct (High Level) station.
Brian Stephenson Collection

Below:
Another regular user of the Widened Lines was the GWR, which worked the trains from Smithfield. Eleven members of GWR's '8750' class 0-6-0PTs were fitted with condensing apparatus for working through to Smithfield, the first being No 8700 of 1931 which was fitted with the equipment in 1932 and, in 1934, renumbered 9700. Its ten contemporaries carried Nos 9701-10 (and condensing gear) from new. Although undated, this picture of No 9704 at Old Oak Common was probably taken very shortly after the locomotive was delivered.
R. M. Casserley Collection

The end of an era

The Metropolitan Railway, the grand pioneer of London's underground railways, saw its independence come to an end on 1 July 1933 when Herbert Morrison's newly-created brainchild, the London Passenger Transport Board, came into existence and took control of not only the Met, but also the District Railway, the Underground and various bus operations. By then, however, virtually all the District had to offer in the way of steam-hauled workings was the hosting of LMSR freight trains on the Hounslow branch, access being by means of the connection at South Acton. For the Metropolitan Railway the final indignity came on 1 November 1937 when all steam workings north of Rickmansworth, including the goods workings on the whole of the Aylesbury line, were transferred to the LNER.

The demise of the Metropolitan Railway was a significant low-point in the story of steam on the Underground. Nevertheless, it had relatively little immediate effect on the number of steam-hauled workings which remained either on the LPTB map or on lines which were to be appended to the map in the coming years. Indeed, steam was far from finished.

Below:
The District Railway retained just six of its 54 Beyer Peacock 4-4-0Ts after electrification. Of those six, only Nos 33 and 34 lasted any length of time, the former being withdrawn in 1925 but the latter surviving until 1932. During its final years, No 34's duties involved the hauling of stores vans and ballast wagons at night when the electric current was switched off. Here, it is seen modelling the 'UNDERGROUND' logo at Lillie Bridge on 12 August 1926.
H. C. Casserley

Bottom:
In 1930 a pair of Hunslet 0-6-0Ts were purchased for departmental duties on the District Railway. They became Nos L30/31 and survived until the early 1960s. This picture shows No L30 at Lillie Bridge depot on 28 May 1931.
H. C. Casserley

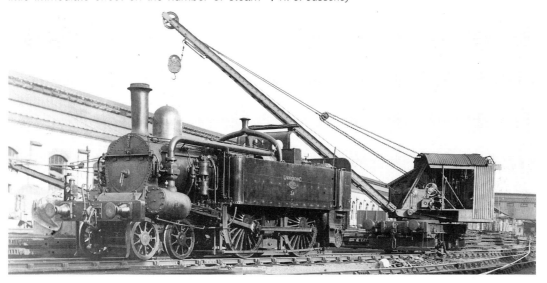

Above:

In 1922, the District Railway acquired a diminutive 0-4-2ST for light shunting duties. It is believed that the locomotive was bought second-hand, but the Kerr Stuart works plate cites a building date of 1922 which might indicate that Kerr Stuart had rebuilt the engine prior to resale to the District. The locomotive survived to be taken into London Transport stock as No L34.
Ian Allan Library

Below:

District Line electric services were not extended to Upminster until 1932. This pre-electrification picture shows ex-LT&SR 4-4-2T No 2147 on an Ealing-Southend working near Hornchurch.
F. R. Hebron/Rail Archive Stephenson

4

Life with
London Transport

Within a few short years of the Metropolitan Railway's demise, World War 2 broke out. The London area suffered terribly during the war and, of course, a vast number of railway installations were affected, either directly or indirectly. In the spirit of the day, however, a return to 'business as usual' was normally brought about with remarkable alacrity although naturally there were many long-term casualties. Among the rail services which were affected were those of the LPTB and the LMSR on the West London line, bomb damage necessitating a suspension in October 1940. Most Southern Railway services between Kensington (Addison Road) and Clapham Junction were cut at the same time.

At Moorgate, the war brought about a suspension of train services until 1 January 1940, from which date a reduced service was introduced. However, on 4 January 1941 a complete suspension was once again enforced and lasted until 1 October 1945. Because of bomb damage sustained at Moorgate, the passenger services nominally terminated at Aldersgate, the locomotives continuing to Moorgate only for turning purposes; it was 6 May 1946 before reconstructed bay platforms at Moorgate were officially opened to traffic. The change of arrangements for Moorgate services had a knock-on effect at King's Cross. As the Metropolitan's original station at King's Cross had been resited to the west of the Widened Lines junction, LMSR trains had no underground stopping place at King's Cross on their way to Aldersgate. The solution was to reopen part of the old Metropolitan station at King's Cross, complete with a separate entrance and booking office at 261 Pentonville Road, for rush hour workings.

With the necessity for wartime economies, the Pullman car service on the former Metropolitan 'main line' between Baker Street and Aylesbury was withdrawn on 7 October 1939. It was considered that a maximised passenger capacity in a standard coaching formation was essential, and so the Pullman cars simply had to go. Normal first-class accommodation was nevertheless retained on the Aylesbury route, and that service was one of only two on the former Metropolitan and District lines which did not lose first-class facilities as from February 1940.

The ex-Metropolitan lines

When the steam workings north of Rickmansworth had been transferred to the LNER in November 1937, so had 18 ex-Metropolitan Railway main line locomotives. Eventually, though, the LNER displaced the former Met engines with its own standard steeds including 'V1' class 2-6-2Ts and, from 1948, 'L1' class 2-6-4Ts. By the end of 1948, 16 'L1s' were allocated to Neasden along with 11 veteran 'N5' 0-6-2Ts and three ex-GCR 'C13' 4-4-2Ts, the last-named type having returned to the London area after an absence of some twenty years.

Neasden depot was the main source of motive power for the section beyond Rickmansworth, although locomotives were regularly out-stationed at Aylesbury. By the mid-1950s LMSR-type 2-6-4Ts had started to share the Aylesbury turns with the 'L1s' and the time allowed for the locomotive change at Rickmansworth was, by then, just four minutes. During that period, four carriage sets for the steam-hauled services were usually stabled at Neasden, three at Aylesbury and one at Wendover. A further set, which had been built in 1898, converted for EMU operation in 1906, then re-adapted for push-pull work, was kept at Chesham for duties on the short branch from Chalfont & Latimer, a Neasden-based 'N5' 0-6-2T often being sub-shedded at Chesham for working the line.

Quadrupling of the Aylesbury line had reached Harrow-on-the-Hill in 1932, but work beyond there was interrupted by the war and did not resume until 1958. Simultaneously, electrification was extended from Rickmansworth to Amersham, the Chesham branch being included in the scheme. The Chesham branch succumbed to electrification in September 1960, the last steam workings operating on the 11th of that month. Right to the very end, the push-pull workings on the line had been operated, it is believed, with some of the oldest standard gauge coaches in regular service in Britain. Perhaps predictably, the veteran carriages attracted the attention of preservationists, and five of the six subsequently found new owners, four going to the Bluebell Railway in Sussex.

Electrification finally reached Amersham one year later. On 9 September 1961 the last scheduled steam-hauled passenger train ran on London Transport metals, and the event was duly witnessed by crowds of enthusiasts. Two days later, on Monday 11 September, the all-electric service to Amersham was inaugurated and, with the passing of the section beyond there to British Railways, Amersham became the extremity of the London Transport network.

In November 1937, 18 ex-Metropolitan Railway locomotives became LNER stock. The Met's handsome 'H' class 4-4-4Ts were redesignated the 'H2' class by the LNER and renumbered 6415-22. Here, No 6417 (ex-Met No 105) is seen at Neasden in the late 1930s. *C. C. B. Herbert*

Above:
LNER 'B1' 4-6-0 No 1130 of Leicester (GC) shed passes Rickmansworth with a fast train for Marylebone on 13 April 1948. The locomotive awaits renumbering as BR No 61130.
J. C. Flemons

Below:
Edward Thompson's 'L1' 2-6-4Ts made their débuts on the ex-Metropolitan 'main line' in 1948. Two-month-old No E9005 was photographed leaving Aylesbury with a Baker Street train on 12 April 1948. The locomotive's new number of 67706 was applied later that month.
Rev A.W.V.Mace

Top:
'L1' 2-6-4T approaches Rickmansworth with a stopping train from Marylebone on 10 September 1955. London Transport electric locomotive No 10 *W. E. Gladstone* waits in the bay prior to taking over an Aylesbury-Baker Street working.
R. M. Newland

Above:
Ex-LMSR '8P' 4-6-2 No 46201 *Princess Elizabeth* passes Kenton with the down 'Merseyside Express' in July 1951. The electrified tracks of the Bakerloo Line are on the right.
C. R. L. Coles

Bottom right:
Electrification reached Amersham in September 1961. Here, Neasden depot's ex-LMSR '4P' 2-6-4T No 42231 is seen entering Amersham in the late 1950s.
Ian Allan Library

Above:

At Willesden Green, 'tube' and non-electrified tracks ran side by side. Ex-LNER 'N7' 0-6-2T No 69689 (the first of the class to be withdrawn) was photographed there in 1951 on a Northolt-Marylebone working.
Ian Allan Library

Left:

A coal train, hauled by '9F' 2-10-0 No 92056, passes through Harrow on 11 March 1957. The Metropolitan Line's electrified tracks are hidden from view behind the platform.
C. R. L. Coles

Above:
Vintage 'Ashbury' coaching stock remained in use on the Chesham branch until the cessation of steam workings in 1960 and, in April 1951, the branch locomotive also displayed an air of antiquity. 'C13' class 4-4-2T No 67418 had been built in 1903 for the Great Central Railway. It was not retired until the end of 1958.
C. R. L. Coles

Below:
The last day of steam working on the Chesham branch was 11 September 1960, and '2MT' No 41284 was in charge of proceedings.
London Transport

The Widened Lines

By the early 1950s Moorgate handled only around 12 or 13 Eastern Region trains each weekday, a far cry from the once prolific Great Northern services. By then, the regular destinations were Hatfield, Hertford North or New Barnet, the Moorgate-High Barnet workings having been discontinued in 1939 prior to electrification. The London Midland Region's sparse contribution to Moorgate's welfare during the early 1950s comprised two trains from St Albans in the mornings and three in the return direction in the evenings. The old LMSR services between Moorgate and Hampstead, East Ham and Barking had disappeared with the outbreak of war.

However, the Widened Lines were certainly not left to gather a film of rust between rush hours. Throughout the day there were goods workings from Ferme Park (ER) and Brent (LMR), via the Widened Lines and Snow Hill, to the SR marshalling yards at Hither Green and Norwood Junction, the LMR outposts of Wandsworth Road and Peckham Rye, and the ER's 'foreign' goods depot at Brockley Lane. In 1951 around 100 freight trains used the Widened Lines route daily.

On the Widened Lines themselves, the Metropolitan Railway's goods depot at Vine Street, which had been served exclusively by electric-hauled trains, had closed in 1936. However, steam workings suffered a set-back with the closure in the same year of the ex-Midland Railway depot at Whitecross Street. Nevertheless, a reasonable flow of freight continued to be handled at the City Goods Depot at Farringdon, where the ground was cobbled up to rail level, until its closure in January 1956. The WR operated to and from Smithfield Goods Depot (closed July 1962), beneath the Central Meat Market, but only westbound trains had direct access to the Widened Lines, eastbound workings having to use the Inner Circle as far as Aldersgate where they were reversed into the depot; of necessity, those WR workings usually operated late at night. Another WR steam working over London Transport electrified lines during the 1950s was an occasional coal train from Westbourne Park to Hammersmith, the return trip being made via the West London line; again, those workings were nocturnal to avoid disruption to normal traffic.

The cross-London freight workings through the Widened Lines and Snow Hill were usually undertaken with the locomotive facing south.

The old Metropolitan station at King's Cross presented a fascinating contrast to its main line counterpart above ground. Here, LMSR '1P' 0-4-4T No 1371 prepares to depart on 24 August 1938. The rebuilding of the station started in the mid-1930s but took many years to complete. Ultimately, a 250ft-long passenger concourse was created by using the site of a defunct bay platform.
H. C. Casserley

Therefore, the return trips to King's Cross and Hornsey were undertaken bunker-first, which at least alleviated the potential danger to crews of flying sparks during the hard climb from the Met to the main line station at King's Cross. Considering that most of the goods trains were loose-coupled, the skill shown in safely negotiating the tortuous curves and gradients on the cross-London line spoke volumes for the footplate crews' expertise.

One unpopular turn which was transferred from Top Shed to Hornsey in the late 1940s was banking duties up the 1 in 39 to Snow Hill, and the vision of an LMSR 'Jinty' 0-6-0T at the head of a southbound train was usually cursed by the ER men as, owing to the small tanks of the 'Jintys', they were normally worked sparingly, thereby leaving the banking engine to do a disproportionate amount of the work. Even on arduous banking duties, the old practice among Top Shed crews of running in non-condensing mode seemed to be perpetuated right through to the 1950s. The last scheduled freight train to use the Widened Lines/Snow Hill route was a diesel-hauled parcels working on 23 March 1969. The rails through Snow Hill were lifted in 1972, but were relaid in 1987 for the new 'Thameslink' passenger services between Bedford and the southeast. An electric service between Luton and Moorgate had been introduced in 1983.

Centre right:
In the 1950s Moorgate still had significant bursts of activity during the rush hours. On 27 July 1956, the 5.22pm to Welwyn is hauled by 'N2' class 0-6-2T No 69583, while '3P' 2-6-2T No 40023 prepares to take on water before its next turn.
H. C. Casserley

Above left:
Condenser-fitted LMSR 2-6-2T No 37 (later BR No 40037) pulls into the old Metropolitan station at King's Cross on 24 August 1938.
H. C. Casserley

Left:
For photographers, Farringdon and High Holborn station (as stated on the London Transport totem) was a sort of miniature Liverpool Street where shafts of sunlight penetrated the glazed sections of the roof to provide atmospheric conditions. It is, however, most unlikely that Henry Fowler had such matters in mind when he created his '3P' 2-6-2Ts in 1930, although No 35 (later BR No 40035) adds to the scene in this picture of 23 August 1947.
H. C. Casserley

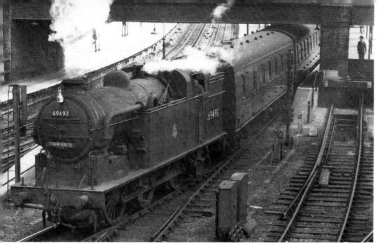

Left:
Steam-hauled workings continued to appear at Moorgate station throughout the 1950s and into the early 1960s. Here, 'N2' class 0-6-2T No 69493 departs from Moorgate in April 1956.
Rail Archive Stephenson

Left:
By the end of the evening rush hour, Moorgate was restored to its air of tranquillity. On 30 March 1962, '3P' 2-6-2T No 40031 brings in the empty stock for the 6.15pm working to Harpenden, but no potential passengers seem to be waiting.
Leslie Sandler

Top right:
'N2' 0-6-2T No 69591 enters Barbican station with a Moorgate-Hatfield train in July 1955.
W. H. R. Godwin

Centre right:
Even some 40 years after the closure of Snow Hill station, the remains of the platform were still visible. Here, 'N1' class 0-6-2T No 69470 passes through Snow Hill with a southbound train in the early 1950s.
Lens of Sutton

Bottom right:
On 23 June 1949, 'N2' No 69506 was required to assist on a Moorgate-Hertford working after the designated engine had failed. The apparent double-header is seen leaving No 16 platform at King's Cross.
Ian Allan Library

Facing page, top:
A heavy Moorgate-Hertford train pulls out of King's Cross behind 'N2' 0-6-2T No 69542.
Ian Allan Library

Facing page, bottom:
Having struggled up the Hotel Curve with a Moorgate-Hatfield train on 26 March 1959, 'N2' No 69535 emerges at No 16 platform of King's Cross (BR) station. It remains a complete mystery why more photographers didn't pay attention to this remarkable corner of King's Cross.
Brian Stephenson

The East London line

The route of the old East London Railway, which ran between Shoreditch and New Cross, continued to handle a fair amount of freight traffic in the early 1950s, much of it being generated at Spitalfields for transfer to the Southern Region. Although a wagon hoist at Spitalfields enabled direct access to the East London line just to the north of Whitechapel, the hoist was rarely used and, instead, trains were usually taken to Liverpool Street for reversing. As with the steam-worked freight services elsewhere on the Underground, those on the East London line were undertaken either at off-peak times or, more usually, at night. The occasional steam-hauled excursion train continued to use the East London line in the 1950s, and enthusiasts were known to seek out such excursions simply for the rare experience of travelling through the Thames Tunnel behind steam.

For many years the only steam-hauled passenger workings on the old East London Railway were specials, this working of 9 April 1955 being a football supporters' train from Shoeburyness to New Cross Gate. The locomotives are condenser-fitted 'J69' 0-6-0Ts Nos 68607 and 68549.
Ian Allan Library

The London Transport Executive

The East London Railway had, at Nationalisation in 1948, passed to the care of the London Transport Executive, as had the other railways previously encompassed by the London Passenger Transport Board. The LTE had also assumed control of the section of the one-time Metropolitan/GCR joint line as far as the southern end of Aylesbury station, the station itself and the route beyond having passed to British Railways. Other lines which had become the responsibility of the LTE included the Chesham and Watford branches, the greater part of the lines to Ealing Broadway and Greenford, and also the former-LNER Northern Heights suburban lines which had, by then, been served by extensions of the Northern Line.

Top:
During the 1950s, steam traction managed to coexist peacefully with London Transport electric stock on the Barking/Upminster line. Here, Stanier '3P' 2-6-2T No 40142 enters Barking with the 1.50pm ex-Kentish Town. The original station at Barking comprised two platforms at a level crossing, but had been twice rebuilt by 1932. Further rebuilding of the station took place between 1959 and 1962.
S. Creer

Above:
Ealing Broadway and Greenford were on separate 'Underground' lines, but the Western Region provided a service between the two. Here, '54XX' class 0-6-0PT No 5414 approaches Greenford with a train from Ealing on 25 September 1954.
C. R. L. Coles

Left:
On 29 March 1959, '3P' 2-6-2T No 40111 of Kentish Town shed descends into Barking station. The construction work on the left of the picture is the LTE flyover. *Frank Church*

The West London Railway

Only short sections of the old WLR route ever became appendages of the Underground map, but the line was nevertheless an important component in the story of Inner London's railways. The line saw a wide variety of steam-hauled workings until the 1960s, many through passenger trains between the north and the south of England continuing to be routed via the WLR, with transfer freight workings between the LMR and the SR contributing a great deal to the activity on the line. Furthermore, if diversions were in operation at any of London's main line termini, Kensington station was an obvious choice as an alternative starting and finishing point for some of the affected long-distance trains. This was the case on two particular occasions in the 1960s, firstly during the reconstruction of Euston station

and, later, when the approaches to Paddington were being rearranged. However, the once-prolific local passenger services to, from or through Kensington had almost disappeared after World War 2, only a handful of peak-time trains to and from Clapham Junction remaining in the timetables.

Kensington (Addison Road) was formally retitled Olympia in 1946, but that was mainly for the benefit of passengers on London Transport's electric services from Earls Court. In the mid-1960s, it became a terminus for Motorail services, cars and passengers being transported to and from Fishguard Harbour and St Austell every day during the holiday periods. The other side of the coin was that, in 1968, the station lost its milk traffic, early morning milk trains having been a feature of the station's life seemingly since its opening.

Above left:
The route of the old West London Railway continued to host steam-hauled trains during the 1950s. Here, ex-SE&CR 'C' class 0-6-0 No 31716 passes through West Brompton with a southbound special.
Real Photographs/Ian Allan Library

Left:
During the 1950s the lines through the disused West London Extension Railway platforms alongside West Brompton Underground station provided occasional entertainment for waiting 'tube' passengers. In this undated picture, SR 'W' class 2-6-4T No 31922 hauls a northbound transfer freight.
Ian Allan Library

Above:

Former LB&SCR Atlantic No 32425 *Trevose Head* was photographed passing through Kensington (Addison Road) with a northbound train on 18 August 1956. The locomotive, which is seen wearing the 75A shedplate of Brighton depot, regularly performed on Hastings-Manchester workings as far as Willesden until its withdrawal just a few weeks after this picture was taken.

R. C. Riley

Below:

A northbound transfer freight, with 'Black Five' No 45025 sporting the special three-lamp headcode, approaches Addison Road on 6 October 1951.

E. D. Bruton

Ongar to Epping, and the Hainault Loop

By the 1950s scheduled steam-hauled passenger services over London Transport tracks were a severely endangered species. Among the few such enigmatic workings were those on the Epping branch, which had been opened throughout by the Great Eastern Railway on 24 April 1865 and had passed to the LNER at the Grouping in 1923. The LNER, in conjunction with the LPTB, had started to electrify the line in the late 1930s and, after the hiatus of the war years, a new 'tube' link to Leytonstone finally opened on 5 May 1947. On 25 September 1949, Central Line electric trains started working right through to Epping.

The final part of the line, that between Epping and Ongar, was not electrified until 18 November 1957 and so, for a little over eight years, steam still ruled on that section. The single-track Epping-Ongar section was worked on a push-pull basis with an early LNER bogie set and a former-GER 'F5' class 2-4-2T or, occasionally, an 'N7' class 0-6-2T out-stationed at the small shed at Epping. Despite the official total conversion to electric traction in 1957, steam locomotives continued to surface occasionally on early morning Liverpool Street-Ongar passenger trains.

Along the Ongar branch, the Hainault Loop diverges at Leytonstone and rejoins it north of Woodford. It follows much of the course of what had originally been known as as the Fairlop Loop, a line that had been built by the GER and

THE HAINAULT LOOP
AND ITS CONNECTIONS

LONDON TRANSPORT (EX·GER)
L T NEW LINES
ABANDONED (EX·GER)
B R EASTERN REGION (EX·GER)
GOODS/COAL DEPOTS

To Epping and Ongar
Original terminus closed 1865
Loughton
Buckhurst Hill
Roding Valley (Formerly Roding Valley Halt; opened by LNER 1930)
Chigwell
Grange Hill
Woodford
Hainault (Closed by GER 1908; reopened by LNER 1930)
Fairlop
South Woodford
Barkingside
Newbury Park
Wanstead
Redbridge
Gants Hill
To Colchester
Leytonstone
To Stratford
Seven Kings
Ilford
To Stratford

Right:
Ex-GER 'F5' class 2-4-2T No 67200 departs from Ongar with the 2.43pm push-pull working to Epping on 28 April 1956. Some 18 months later, Central Line electric trains reached Ongar.
Philip J. Kelley

Left:
The Hainault loop and its connections.

had opened to goods traffic on 20 April 1903 and to passengers on 1 May of that year. Holden 2-4-2Ts or 0-6-0Ts and, later, Hill's 'N7' class 0-6-2Ts had provided the motive power. The southern end of the loop was completely realigned by the end of 1947 and the entire loop was electrifed by 21 November 1948, thereby permitting access by Central Line tube trains.

During the war, some five miles of the partly-completed tunnel under Wanstead had been used as an aircraft factory employing around 2,000 people. In common with the closely-asso-ciated Epping/Ongar branch, the Hainault Loop (as it became known) accommodated regular locomotive-hauled freight trains until 1965, ex-GER 'J15' 0-6-0s being used prior to the takeover by diesels in the final few years. On the Hainault Loop, the latter-day goods workings comprised three each week from Stratford to Newbury Park while, on the Ongar line, coal was delivered in ever-decreasing quantities to yards at six of the stations until the end of 1965.

Above:
The two-coach Ongar-Epping shuttle was worked by 'F5' class 2-4-2T No 67203 on 25 June 1956. Here, it is seen approaching Epping on the soon-to-be electrified section.
G. Clarke

Below:
On the same day, 'F5' class 2-4-2T No 67203 takes on water at Epping prior to taking the two-coach push-pull shuttle to Ongar.
G. Clarke

The Northern Heights

The other 'tube' lines which accommodated steam-hauled services, albeit freight ones, during the 1950s were the old Great Northern branches to High Barnet and Edgware although, on the latter, the section beyond Mill Hill East was never to become part of the London Transport map. As early as 1903, the GNR had proposed the electrification of those branches and also the Alexandra Palace branch, and similar plans had reappeared with regularity during subsequent years. However, it took a joint LNER/LPTB venture of 1935 to achieve positive steps towards the much-debated electrification, the new scheme involving an extension of the Northern Line 'tube' from Archway to Highgate and a junction with the ex-GNR branch at East Finchley.

The electrification to High Barnet was completed on 14 April 1940, although steam traction was not entirely ousted from passenger workings until March 1941. On 18 May 1941 electric services commenced as far as Mill Hill East on the Edgware line, the intention of continuing the electrification into Edgware not being formally abandoned until 1954. Similarly, the electrification of the Alexandra Palace branch was never completed, despite the laying of conductor rails. Freight services continued to operate regularly to High Barnet until 1 October 1961 and sporadically to Mill Hill East until 2 March 1964. The ubiquitous 'N2' class 0-6-2Ts performed haulage duties until the end of November 1960, after which trip-cock fitted Class 15 diesels took over. As far as can be determined, the last appearance of a steam locomotive on the Northern Heights branches was that of 'N2' No 69568 which hauled an LCGB special to High Barnet on 2 September 1961.

The 0-6-2Ts had been the long-standing regulars on Northern Heights duties, although the branches had over the years seen a reasonable variety of motive power. In the early 1900s, GNR 0-8-2Ts had been tried on Edgware-Moorgate Street services, but had proved too cumbersome to be handled comfortably at the latter point. LNER Sentinel and Clayton steam railcars had been used in the late 1920s and early 1930s while, at the other end of the scale, the working of a 'K2' 2-6-0 through to Edgware had not been unknown.

Proposed and actual electrification of ex-GNR 'Northern Heights' lines.

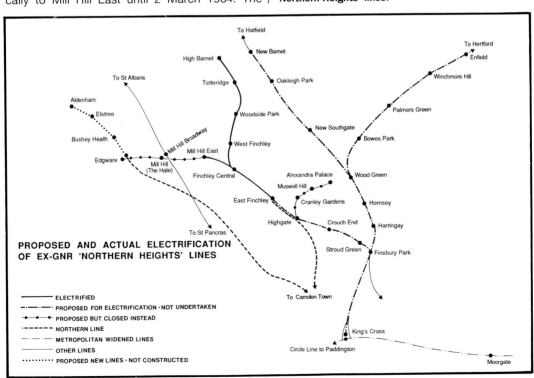

PROPOSED AND ACTUAL ELECTRIFICATION
OF EX-GNR 'NORTHERN HEIGHTS' LINES

—————— ELECTRIFIED
—·—·—·— PROPOSED FOR ELECTRIFICATION - NOT UNDERTAKEN
•—•—•—• PROPOSED BUT CLOSED INSTEAD
– – – – NORTHERN LINE
——————— METROPOLITAN WIDENED LINES
—————— OTHER LINES
············· PROPOSED NEW LINES - NOT CONSTRUCTED

Above:
The extension of the Northern Line 'tube' to High Barnet was completed in April 1940. This picture shows how far the work at East Finchley station had progressed by August the previous year.
London Transport

Below:
Although it was proposed to entend the Northern Line 'tube' beyond Mill Hill East to Edgware, the former point was the furthest ever reached by electrification.

Consequently, The Hale station, which had been cumbersomely renamed 'Mill Hill (for The Hale)' in March 1928, only narrowly avoided becoming a feature of the London Underground map. While Mill Hill East profited from its new electric connection, the fortunes of the steam-worked section beyond there to Edgware dwindled and passenger services were withdrawn from that section on 11 September 1939. On 5 June 1937, LNER 'N2' 0-6-2T No 4738 (later BR No 69517) was photographed arriving at The Hale.
H. C. Casserley

Below:
The laying of conductor rails was about as far as things ever went with the proposed electrification of the Alexandra Palace branch. The locomotive seen on this 'Ally Pally' push-pull working is ex-GNR 'C12' 4-4-2T No 7374. The date was probably around 1950 as that locomotive and classmate No 7356 were not fitted for push-pull operation until 1948/49; No 7374 did not receive its BR number (No 67374) until as late as February 1951.
P. Ransome-Wallis

Bottom:
The electrification of the line through Stroud Green first came under discussion by the Great Northern Railway in 1903. Nothing came of that scheme, and the joint LNER/LPTB plans of 1935 to extend the Northern Line 'tube' to the Northern Heights avoided Stroud Green only by a mile or so. This picture shows 'N2' class 0-6-2T No 2666 (later BR No 69572) at Stroud Green with a High Barnet working in June 1939.
W. S. Garth/Rail Archive Stephenson

Steam's other duties

On former District Railway metals, the only regular revenue-earning working hauled by steam during the early 1950s was a daily freight from Brent to the old Midland Railway coal depot adjacent to High Street, Kensington. Motive power usually took the form of a '3F' 0-6-0T which, despite being fitted with the obligatory condensing apparatus, undertook most of its journey in the open.

The District's old depot at Lillie Bridge, where London Transport's steam locomotives were serviced and repaired, usually housed a couple of LT's remaining steam locomotives. Their duties were almost entirely departmental, with ballast workings predominating. Nevertheless, three regular steam-hauled engineers' workings were operated from Lillie Bridge almost to the very end. One was a daytime run to Acton Yard, the others being night trips to Neasden via Rayners Lane and Upminster via the southern part of the Inner Circle.

The majority of LT's steam locomotives lived at Neasden, one of that depot's well-known departmental runs of later years being to the spoil tip on the Watford branch. During the 1950s, the BR shed at Neasden was occasionally unable to muster a suitable steed for Sunday passenger services to Aylesbury, and a Neasden-based LT steam locomotive was consequently given an airing. When, in 1956, London Transport addressed the need for replacement locomotives it was considered that, due to the small number of hours which the locomotives were required to work, diesel locomotives would be an uneconomical proposition. Consequently, an ex-GWR 0-6-0PT was purchased and, over the next seven years, twelve similar engines were acquired. London Transport retained three of its 0-6-0PTs until June 1971, almost three years after British Railways had converted to characterless internal-combustion machines. The final steam working on 'Underground' metals was on 6 June 1971, although steam-hauled enthusiasts' specials have been operated in recent years.

Considering that the electrification of existing Metropolitan and District Railway lines in and around London had been virtually completed by 1906, it was remarkable that steam-hauled workings on what later became 'Underground' lines continued for another 65 years. As we have seen, the workings of later years had somewhat restricted spheres of operation and, in many cases, were conducted either away from public areas or when most people were fast asleep. Fortunately, though, such activities seemed to act as the proverbial magnet for railway historians and photographers and, consequently, their memories and images are well recorded.

Former Metropolitan Railway 'E' class 0-4-4T No 77 ultimately became No L46 in London Transport's departmental stock. During the late 1940s and early 1950s it was not unusual for one of the ex-Metropolitan steam locomotives to act as standby on the Aylesbury line on Sundays, and No L46 was photographed waiting for its chance of glory at Rickmansworth on 7 April 1947.
H. C. Casserley

On 22 September 1957 ex-Metropolitan 'E' class 0-4-4T No L46 was booked for an SLS special. Here, it is seen at Hammersmith.
R. F. Roberts

Centre left:
The Metropolitan's four 'F' class 0-6-2Ts, Nos 90-93, became Nos L49-52 in London Transport departmental stock. During bridge renewal work at Pinner on 29 May 1954, No L49 was used to haul the train carrying the girders of the old bridge.
C. R. L. Coles

Below:
Ex-Metropolitan 'F' class 0-6-2T became LT No L52, and was photographed at Farringdon on 23 May 1954 having brought the breakdown train from Neasden. The locomotive was cut up at Neasden in July 1964.
LCGB/Ken Nunn Collection

Above:
Two Hunslet 0-6-0Ts were bought by the District Railway in 1930 and eventually became Nos L30/31 in London Transport stock. Here, No L30 is seen at Olympia (formerly Addison Road) on 2 January 1952. The locomotive was unceremoniously cut up at Neasden in July 1964.
Ian Allan Library

Below left:
London Transport's Hunslet 0-6-0T No L31 runs round its permanent way train at Edgware Road station on 6 November 1960. *Ian Allan Library*

Above right:
A Kerr Stuart 0-4-2ST was acquired by the District Railway in 1922 and later became London Transport No L34. *London Transport*

Bottom right:
In 1956 London Transport first developed its taste for ex-GWR '57XX' class 0-6-0PTs, the first two being purchased to replace ex-Metropolitan 'E' class 0-4-4Ts Nos L49/51. Thirteen 0-6-0PTs were bought by the LTE by 1963, details being:

BR No	to LT	LT No	Wdn
7711	10/56	L90	10/61
5752	2/57	L91	11/60
5786	4/58	L92	–/69
7779	10/58	L93	12/67
7752	11/59	L94	6/71
5764	5/60	L95	6/71
5757	12/60	L91	12/67
7741	12/61	L96	12/66
7760	12/61	L90	6/71
7749	9/62	L97	9/68
7739	11/62	L98	11/68
7715	5/63	L99	1/70
5775	7/63	L89	1/70

No L95 was photographed hauling a permanent way train at Farringdon on 23 June 1968. The locomotive was sold to the Severn Valley Railway and subsequently restored to its GWR condition complete with the original number of 5764.
Brian Lowe

Left:
The usual practice was for two of the LT steam locomotives to live at Lillie Bridge, and the others at Neasden. Here, No L95 is seen shunting at Lillie Bridge on 23 January 1970.
J. H. Cooper-Smith

Below:
The last ex-GWR 0-6-0PT to be purchased by the LTE was No 5775, which became No L89. Like No L95, it was later acquired by preservationists (in this case, the Keighley & Worth Valley Railway) and restored to its GWR condition. Here, it is seen approaching South Ealing with an Acton-Northfields train on 2 July 1969.
D. A. Idle

Above:
0-6-0PT No L94 was another LT locomotive to have been preserved in its original GWR guise. Its current owner is the Gloucestershire & Warwickshire Railway. In this picture of 4 October 1970, the handful of passengers waiting for a 'tube' train at Farringdon seem generally unimpressed by the sight of an ex-GWR steam locomotive at the head of a permanent way train.
David M. Scudamore

Below:
A regular turn performed by London Transport steam locomotives was the run to Watford Tip. 0-6-0PT No L99 was photographed at Wembley Park during a snow shower on 12 February 1969 *en route* to the tip.
John H. Bird

On 12 May 1969, 0-6-0PT No L99 takes on water at Watford having reversed in readiness to complete its journey to the tip.
John H. Bird

Centre right:
A returning Watford Tip train passes through Pinner on its way back to Neasden on 7 August 1969. The locomotive is 0-6-0PT No L95.
A. D. K. Young

Below:
The empty spoil train passes through North Harrow on its way back from Watford Tip to Neasden on 12 May 1969. 0-6-0PT No L99 is in charge.
John H. Bird

Above:
On 1 October 1961 ex-Metropolitan 'E' class 0-4-4T No L44 was used to haul the Southern Counties Touring Society special from Stanmore to New Cross Gate. It was photographed near Surrey Docks station on the old East London Railway.
Ian Allan Library

Below:
One of the participants in the Metropolitan Railway's Centenary Parade of 23 May 1963 was 'E' class 0-4-4T No L44, built at Neasden in 1896. Behind the locomotive is restored milk van No 3 and the four ex-Metropolitan coaches of 1898-1900 which had been used on the Chesham branch until only a couple of years previously.
W. H. R. Godwin

The last steam working on the Underground (apart from preservation specials of recent years) occurred on 6 June 1971. It was hauled by 0-6-0PT No L94 and, as clearly evidenced in this splendid photograph, attracted more attention than a permanent way train would normally have merited.
Gary Merrin